Writing Preparation and Practice

2

Karen Blanchard   **Christine Root**

PEARSON
Longman

D1088051

Writing Preparation and Practice 2

Writing Preparation and Practice 2 has been adapted from *Ready to Write, Third Edition,* by Fanny Safier. Ms. Safier has taught literature and composition at the secondary and college levels. She has more than thirty years of experience in editing and developing middle school and secondary language arts programs.

Pearson Education, 10 Bank Street, White Plains, NY 10606

Staff credits: The people who made up the **Writing Preparation and Practice 2** team, representing editorial, production, design, and manufacturing, are Danielle Belfiore, Nancy Flaggman, Gosia Jaros-White, Dana Klinek, Laura Le Dréan, Melissa Leyva, Paula Van Ells, and Pat Wosczyk.

Cover image: Marjory Dressler Photo Graphics
Text composition: Rainbow Graphics
Text font: 11/14 ITC Franklin Gothic Book
Illustrations: James Yamasaki
Text art: Kenneth Batelman: pp. 28, 39, 41, 43, 44, 59, 61, 62, 76, 113; Paula Williams: pp. 6, 49, 122; Rainbow Graphics: pp. 58, 64, 65, 66, 74, 75, 85, 87, 91, 93, 99, 100, 101, 102, 103, 104, 121, 123, 124, 126, 135, 147, 149, 150, 151, 153, 157, 158, 160, 161–162, 163
Text and photo credits: pp. 5, 49, 145: Paula Williams, Lisa Ghiozzi; p. 58: Copyright © 2005 by The New York Times Co. Reprinted with permission.; p. 61: Reprinted with permission from Open Doors: 2001, The Institute of International Education; p. 62: Adapted from *The Complete Book of Running,* by James F. Fixx, © 1977 by Random House, Inc.; p. 64: Copyright © 2005 by The Associated Press. Reprinted with permission.; p. 138: PEANUTS reprinted by permission of United Feature Syndicate, Inc.

Library of Congress Cataloging-in-Publication Data

Blanchard, Karen Lourie

    Writing preparation and practice/ Karen Blanchard and Christine Root.— 1st ed.
        p. cm.
    ISBN 0-13-238002-1 (student book 1: alk. paper)—ISBN 0-13-199556-1 (student book 2: alk. paper)—ISBN 0-13-243553-5 (student book 3: alk. paper) 1. English language—Textbooks for foreign speakers. 2. English language—Rhetoric—Problems, exercises, etc. 3. Report writing—Problems, exercises, etc. I. Root, Christine Baker II. Title.

PE1128.B5875 2006
808'.0428—dc22

                                     2006005371

ISBN: 0-13-199556-1

Printed in the United States of America
3 4 5 6 7 8 9 10—VHG—10 09 08 07

CONTENTS

Introduction......iv

CHAPTER **1** Organizing: The Key to Good Writing......1

CHAPTER **2** Understanding Paragraphs......9

CHAPTER **3** Organizing Information by Time......23

CHAPTER **4** Organizing Information by Order of Importance......31

CHAPTER **5** Organizing Information by Space......39

CHAPTER **6** Following the Writing Process......47

CHAPTER **7** Supporting the Main Idea......55

CHAPTER **8** Giving Instructions......67

CHAPTER **9** Writing Descriptions......79

CHAPTER **10** Expressing an Opinion......92

CHAPTER **11** Comparing and Contrasting......105

CHAPTER **12** Writing About Causes and Effects......128

CHAPTER **13** Writing Personal and Business Letters......148

CHAPTER **14** Writing Summaries......159

Answer Key......169

INTRODUCTION

Writing Preparation and Practice 2 is a high-beginning and low-intermediate writing skills textbook for English language learners. With this text, students will learn to write well and achieve more complete English proficiency by learning and practicing writing skills simultaneously with other English language skills. Students are supplied with the basic vocabulary; they are also taught explicitly how the English language organizes information. With these tools, students are able to write on a variety of provocative and sophisticated topics.

APPROACH

Writing Preparation and Practice 2 gets students writing early in their second language acquisition experience. By providing them with a wide variety of stimulating writing topics and exercises that go beyond sentence manipulation drills, the book encourages students to bring their own ideas and talent to the writing process. With a focus on the process of writing paragraphs, students learn, step by step, the organizational principles that will help them express themselves efficiently in English. They also learn to apply these principles to a variety of rhetorical formats.

The activities in the *Writing Preparation and Practice* series are designed to encourage students to think independently as well as provide them with many opportunities to share ideas with their classmates, thus creating a more dynamic learning environment. To this end, collaborative writing and peer feedback activities are included in all chapters. In addition, great care has been taken to maintain an appropriate level of vocabulary and complexity of sentence structure for high-beginning and low-intermediate students so that the explanations, directions, and readings are easily accessible.

FEATURES

- attention to different patterns of organization through the use of *model paragraphs*
- guidance and practice in recognizing and writing the *parts of the paragraph*
- guided practice in each stage of the paragraph writing process, including specific techniques for *prewriting*, *writing*, and *revising*
- numerous and varied *paragraph-writing* opportunities
- attention to *style* through presentations and activities on coherence, transitions, and the use of signal words
- editing practice in error correction and proofreading (an answer key for this section is at the end of this book)
- additional individual practice in paragraph-writing skills

Together, the approach and features of *Writing Preparation and Practice 2* work to guide students to a higher level of confidence and proficiency.

CHAPTER 1

Organizing: The Key to Good Writing

Writing can be difficult even in your own language. In a new language, writing can be even more difficult. The good news is that writing involves skills that you can learn, practice, and master. As you work through this book, you will learn and practice skills you need to become a good writer in English.

Organization is the key to good writing. Different languages organize ideas differently. In this chapter, you will begin to learn how to organize information in English so that you can write effective paragraphs.

Organizing by Grouping

Look at the following list of places.

South America	Asia
New York City	Tokyo
Italy	Mexico
Korea	Europe
Istanbul	

This list can be organized by dividing it into three groups.

A	**B**	**C**
South America	Italy	New York City
Asia	Korea	Istanbul
Europe	Mexico	Tokyo

Now answer the following questions.

1. What do all the places in group A have in common?

They are continents.

2. What do all the places in group B have in common?

3. What do all the places in group C have in common?

Each group can be further organized by giving it a name.

A **CONTINENTS**	**B** **COUNTRIES**	**C** **CITIES**
South America	Italy	New York City
Asia	Korea	Istanbul
Europe	Mexico	Tokyo

ORGANIZING LISTS

A Organize each list of words by dividing it into three groups. Put similar ideas together and give each group a name. One list has been done for you.

1. ~~Sunday~~   winter
January   spring
February   ~~Friday~~
summer   December
~~Tuesday~~

A	B	C
Name: *days*	Name: _____	Name: _____
Sunday	_____	_____
Tuesday	_____	_____
Friday	_____	_____

2. jet   truck
bus   helicopter
boat   submarine
car   ship
airplane

A	B	C
Name: _____	Name: _____	Name: _____
_____	_____	_____
_____	_____	_____
_____	_____	_____

3. Spanish   chemistry
calculus   Arabic
biology   geometry
algebra   physics
Japanese

A	B	C
Name: _____	Name: _____	Name: _____
_____	_____	_____
_____	_____	_____
_____	_____	_____

(continued on next page)

4. ring   glasses
    hat   mittens
    shoes   boots
    socks   headband
    gloves

    A   **B**   **C**

Name: _____   Name: _____   Name: _____

_____   _____   _____

_____   _____   _____

_____   _____   _____

B **Often there is more than one way to organize things. Study the list.**

    hot chocolate   pork   tea
    roast beef   carrots   spinach
    milk   soda   juice
    potatoes   chicken coffee

1. **First divide the list into *two* groups and give each group a name.**

        A   **B**

Name: _____   Name: _____

_____   _____

_____   _____

_____   _____

_____   _____

_____   _____

2. **Now divide each group again. Give each new group a name.**

        A   **B**

Name: _____   Name: _____

_____   _____

_____   _____

_____   _____

Name: _____   Name: _____

_____   _____

_____   _____

_____   _____

Can you think of something else to add to each group?

Topics

When you organized the lists, you put similar items together. You also gave each group a name. The name is the topic.

CHOOSING A TOPIC

One word in each list is more general than the others. This word is the topic of the list. Circle the topic.

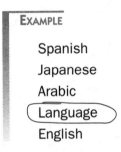

EXAMPLE

Spanish
Japanese
Arabic
(Language)
English

A	B	C	D	E
Honda	tennis	Lincoln	occupations	flowers
cars	soccer	presidents	dentist	trees
Volvo	sports	Clinton	teacher	vegetation
Mercedes	baseball	Kennedy	lawyer	plants
Ford	football	Bush	engineer	grass

WRITING A TOPIC

Write a topic for each list.

A	B	C
_____	_____	_____
Atlantic	four	apple
Pacific	seventeen	orange
Indian	fifty	banana
	three hundred	peach

Irrelevant Information

When you organize your information into groups, it is important to recognize when something does not belong. When something does not belong, it is called *irrelevant*.

IDENTIFYING IRRELEVANT INFORMATION

A **Cross out the item in each group that does not belong.**

EXAMPLE

2   4   6   ~~5~~

1.

2.

3.

4.

B Cross out the word in each of the following groups that does not belong. Then write a topic for each list.

food
candy
chicken
~~flowers~~
vegetables

1. _____
green
dress
yellow
blue

2. _____
Pennsylvania
Philadelphia
Florida
California

3. _____
desk
chair
table
book

4. _____
Spanish
Turkish
Chinese
Modern

5. _____
physics
swimming
biology
chemistry

6. _____
February
Wednesday
April
June

7. _____
computer
telephone
fax machine
washing machine

8. _____
tire
horn
steering wheel
Volkswagen

C Cross out the sentence in each group that does not belong.

Topic: It is interesting to visit foreign countries.
a. You can meet new people.
b. You can eat different kinds of food.
c. ~~It is expensive.~~
d. You can see the way other people live.

1. **Topic:** There is a lot to do in New York City.
   a. There are many museums to see.
   b. It is the cultural center of the United States.
   c. The subways are dirty.
   d. There are many kinds of restaurants.

2. **Topic:** People prefer small cars for a number of reasons.
   a. They are cheaper to buy.
   b. They use less gas than bigger cars.
   c. They are easier to park.
   d. Some small cars do not have enough legroom.

(continued on next page)

3. **Topic:** Different people spend their free time in different ways.
   a. A lot of people spend their free time going to movies.
   b. The price of movies has increased recently.
   c. Some people like to read.
   d. Many people enjoy sports.
   e. Some people prefer to listen to music.

4. **Topic:** Smoking cigarettes is a bad habit.
   a. It is expensive.
   b. It may cause cancer.
   c. There are many kinds of cigarettes.
   d. The smoke often bothers other people.
   e. Burning cigarettes cause fires.

CLASS ACTIVITY

Make a list of all the people in your class. Organize the list by dividing the people into groups. There are many ways to do this. For example, you can have one group for females and another for males. How many ways can you think of to organize your classmates? Remember that all members of a group should have something in common.

On Your Own

1. Make a list of things you have to do this weekend. Organize the items on your list into groups. Give each group a name.

2. Make a list of all the things you *should* do when you are learning a new language. Make another list of all the things you *shouldn't* do.

CHAPTER 2
Understanding Paragraphs

Most English writing is organized into paragraphs. A paragraph is a group of sentences that develops one main idea. It usually begins with a sentence that states the main idea. This sentence is called the topic sentence. The other sentences in the paragraph explain the main idea. They add details and give support. These sentences are called supporting sentences. Sometimes paragraphs also have a concluding sentence. It is the last sentence of the paragraph.

Read the model paragraph and study the parts.

>   The students in the class come from many different parts of the world. Some are from European countries such as France, Spain, and Italy. Others are from Middle Eastern countries like Saudi Arabia and Israel. Still other students were born in Asian countries, including Japan and Korea. The largest number of students are from Latin American countries like Mexico, Venezuela, and Peru. The class is an interesting mix of people from many different countries.

topic sentence

supporting sentences

concluding sentence

A paragraph also needs to be in proper paragraph form. Follow these rules of proper paragraph form.

- Indent the first word of each paragraph.

- Leave margins (space on both sides of the paragraph).

- Begin each sentence with a capital letter.

- End each sentence with a period, question mark, or exclamation point.

- Do not start each new sentence on a new line.

Identifying Parts of a Paragraph

Read the following paragraphs and answer the questions.

1.   There are many reasons why people move. Some move to find better jobs or to advance their careers. Others are attracted to places with better weather. Still others want to move to a place with less crime. Finally, people often want to move to a place with a lower cost of living. For these reasons, every year millions of people pack up and move to new places.

    a. What is the topic sentence?

    _____

    b. How many supporting sentences are there in the paragraph? _____

    c. Is there a concluding sentence? _____

2.   Many women are now employed in jobs that traditionally belonged to men. For example, from 1999 to 2004 alone, the number of female dentists in the United States increased from 16.5 percent to 22.2 percent. Women now work as airline pilots, plumbers, security guards, stockbrokers, and truck drivers. There are many other occupations where the number of women is increasing. It is clear that ideas about traditional male occupations have changed.

a. What is the topic sentence?

_____

b. How many supporting sentences are there in the paragraph? _____

c. Is there a concluding sentence? _____

3. For thousands of years garlic has had many uses. The Romans gave garlic to their slaves for strength and to their soldiers for courage. During the Middle Ages, some people used garlic to keep witches away. In the eighteenth century, garlic was used to cure diseases. Even today, some people believe that eating garlic can prevent colds. Garlic has a long history as a plant that can give health and protection.

a. What is the topic sentence?

_____

b. How many supporting sentences are there in the paragraph? _____

c. Is there a concluding sentence? _____

Topic Sentences

The topic sentence is the most important sentence of a paragraph. It states the main idea and introduces the reader to the topic.

CHOOSING A TOPIC SENTENCE

Choose the best topic sentence for each group of supporting sentences. Write it on the line provided.

EXAMPLE

Skiing is my favorite sport. I usually go skiing every weekend in the winter even though it is expensive. I love the feeling of flying down a mountain. The views are beautiful from the top of a mountain and along the trails. Even the danger of falling and getting hurt can't keep me away from the slopes on a winter day.

a. Skiing is expensive.
b. Skiing is my favorite sport.
c. Skiing is dangerous.

1. _____

North Americans send cards for many occasions. They send cards to family and friends on birthdays and holidays. They also send thank-you cards, get well cards, graduation cards, and congratulation cards. It is very common to buy cards in stores and send them through the mail, but turning on the computer and sending cards over the Internet is also popular.

   a. Sending cards is very popular in North America.
   b. Birthday cards are the most popular kind of card.
   c. It is important to send thank-you cards.

2. _____

I enjoy summer sports like waterskiing and baseball. The weather is usually sunny and hot, so I can go to the beach almost every day. Gardening is my hobby and I spend many summer days working in my garden. Unfortunately, the days pass too quickly in summer.

   a. I like to garden in the summer.
   b. Summer is my favorite season.
   c. Summer is too short.

3. _____

First of all, we need money to repair old roads and build new roads. We also need more money to pay teachers' salaries and to pay for services such as trash collection. Finally, more tax money is needed to give financial help to the poor citizens of the city. It is clear that the city will have serious problems if taxes are not raised soon.

   a. We should raise city taxes.
   b. City taxes are too high.
   c. City taxes pay for new roads.

4. _____

For example, a person can have breakfast in New York, board an airplane, and have dinner in Paris. A businesswoman in London can instantly place an order with a factory in Hong Kong by sending an e-mail. Furthermore, a schoolboy in Tokyo can turn on a TV and watch a baseball game being played in Los Angeles.

   a. Airplanes have changed our lives.
   b. Advances in technology have made the world seem smaller.
   c. E-mail was an important invention.

5. _____

One thing you must consider is the quality of the university's educational program. You also need to think about the school's size and location. Finally, you must be sure to consider the university's tuition to make sure you can afford to go to school there.

   a. It is expensive to attend a university in the United States.
   b. There are several factors to consider when you choose a university to attend.
   c. You should consider getting a good education.

WRITING A TOPIC SENTENCE

Write a topic sentence for each paragraph. Make sure your topic sentence expresses the main idea of the paragraph. Then share your topic sentences with your classmates by writing them on the chalkboard. Discuss the differences.

EXAMPLE

Miami is the perfect place to take a vacation. It is always sunny and warm. The beaches are gorgeous, with soft white sand and beautiful water. There are many fine restaurants in the Miami area, and most of the hotels offer terrific entertainment nightly. It's no wonder that Miami is my first choice for a vacation destination.

1. _____

He has collected stamps and coins ever since he was a child. He is very proud of his valuable collections. Paul also enjoys painting and drawing. Recently he has become interested in gardening. Out of all his hobbies, Paul's favorite one is reading. He usually reads at least one book every week. Paul keeps busy with all of his hobbies.

2. _____

I can't wait to come home from school and eat the delicious meals she has prepared. She is famous for her desserts like peach pie and chocolate soufflé. She is always experimenting with new recipes and trying different ingredients. No one in the world can cook the way my mother does.

3. _____

It never starts in cold weather. The horn and the left turn signal don't work properly. Worst of all, the radio only gets one station and the CD player is completely broken. I wish my family could get a new car.

4. _____

First, and most importantly, the work is very interesting. I get to learn about the behavior and body language of dogs. In addition, dog walking gives me plenty of outdoor exercise. I take each dog for a fifteen-minute walk around the neighborhood. Working as a dog walker has also taught me how to be patient. Last, but not least, the money I earn goes into my savings for college.

5. _____

To start things off, our plane was six hours late. When we finally got to our hotel, we were very disappointed. It was small and dirty. On the third day, my father's wallet was stolen, and he lost all his credit cards. It rained every day except one, and on that day I got a terrible sunburn. All in all, it wasn't a vacation to remember.

Supporting Sentences

The supporting sentences develop the main idea in the topic sentence. They add details to the topic.

RECOGNIZING SUPPORTING SENTENCES

Read the following paragraphs and underline the supporting sentences.

1. Use of the Internet has grown very quickly. Millions of computers are now connected to the Internet and this number keeps growing. In July 2005, the number of Internet users was estimated at more than 938 million. Between 2000 and 2005, world Internet use increased by 160 percent. As time goes on, the Internet is becoming more and more popular.

2. There are many reasons I hate my apartment. The plumbing doesn't work properly and the landlord refuses to fix it. I also have noisy neighbors who keep me up all night. Furthermore, there are so many bugs in my apartment that I could start an insect collection. I really want to move!

3. Vegetables and fruits are an important part of a healthful diet. First, fruits and vegetables are packed with the vitamins and minerals you need to keep your body functioning smoothly. In addition, they give you the carbohydrates you need for energy. Fruits and vegetables have lots of fiber to help your digestive system work properly. Finally, many scientists believe that the nutrients in fruits and vegetables can help fight diseases. If you eat a diet rich in fruits and vegetables, you'll be on the road to better health.

IDENTIFYING TOPIC AND SUPPORTING SENTENCES

Springfield Academy

A **Read the sentences about Springfield Academy, a boarding school for high school students. Some sentences are about the quality of education. Label these *Q*. Some are about the rules of the school. Label these *R*. With some of your classmates, read and discuss all of the sentences.**

1. _____ Springfield Academy is famous for the high quality of its education.

2. _____ Students are not allowed to leave campus without permission.

3. _____ Students are required to wear uniforms.

4. _____ The laboratories have the newest computers and equipment.

5. _____ Stereos and televisions cannot be played after 7:00 P.M.

6. _____ Most of its graduates attend very good universities.

7. _____ Many of the students at Springfield Academy feel that the rules are too strict and old-fashioned.

8. _____ Students who do not maintain a B average are put on probation.

9. _____ The library is one of the finest in the state.

B Now divide the sentences into two groups. Remember to put similar ideas together.

Quality of Education	Rules of the School
_____	_____
_____	_____
_____	_____
_____	_____
_____	_____
_____	_____
_____	_____

One sentence in each group is general enough to be a topic sentence. Find that sentence in each group and circle it.

C Use the sentences in each group to write two paragraphs. Put the topic sentences first. Review the rules of proper paragraph form on page 10.

Quality of Education

_____

_____

_____

_____

_____

_____

_____

_____

San Francisco

A Read the following sentences about San Francisco. Two of the sentences are topic sentences, and the rest are supporting sentences. Write *TS* in front of each topic sentence and *SS* in front of each supporting sentence.

1. _____ San Francisco is usually warm and pleasant during the day.

2. _____ Some of the country's most famous restaurants and hotels are in San Francisco.

3. _____ There are many things to see and do in San Francisco.

4. _____ The city has many interesting tourist attractions.

5. _____ There are many excellent art galleries.

6. _____ The weather in San Francisco is very pleasant.

7. _____ It is never too hot or too cold.

8. _____ The nightlife is exciting.

9. _____ San Francisco has a ballet company, an opera house, and a symphony orchestra.

10. _____ It is cool and breezy at night.

11. _____ The winters are mild and it rarely snows.

B Write the two topic sentences on the lines provided. Then list the relevant supporting sentences under the topic sentences.

Topic Sentence	**Topic Sentence**
_____	_____
_____	_____
Supporting Sentences	**Supporting Sentences**
_____	_____
_____	_____
_____	_____
_____	_____

_____   _____
_____   _____
_____   _____
_____   _____
_____   _____
_____   _____

C Write the sentences from the first group in paragraph form. Remember to indent the first sentence.

_____

_____

_____

_____

_____

D Now write the sentences from the second group in paragraph form.

_____

_____

_____

_____

_____

Irrelevant Sentences

Every supporting sentence in a paragraph must relate to the main idea stated in the topic sentence. A sentence that does not support the main idea does not belong in the paragraph. When a sentence does not belong in a paragraph, it is called an _irrelevant sentence._

Now read this paragraph again. Which sentence does not belong? Cross out the irrelevant sentence.

> The students in the class come from many different parts of the world. Some are from European countries, such as France, Spain, and Italy. Others are from Middle Eastern countries like Saudi Arabia and Israel. Still other students were born in Asian countries, including Japan and Korea. Korean food is delicious. The largest number of students are from Latin American countries like Mexico, Venezuela, and Peru. The class is an interesting mix of people from many different countries.

The main idea of the paragraph is that the students in the class come from many different parts of the world. The fact that Korean food is delicious is true, but it does not support the main idea.

RECOGNIZING IRRELEVANT SENTENCES

There is one irrelevant sentence in each paragraph that follows. Find that sentence and cross it out.

1.   Cats make wonderful house pets. They are very loving and friendly. Cats are also clean. They don't eat much, so they are not expensive. Unfortunately, some people are allergic to their hair. Cats look beautiful and they're fun to have in your home.

2.   There are several ways people can conserve natural resources. One way is to turn off lights and appliances when they are not in use. Another way is to drive cars less. My favorite kind of car is a convertible. People can also insulate their houses better. Finally, by reusing things like bottles and plastic bags, people can reduce the amount of waste. By practicing these simple guidelines, we can save our natural resources.

3.   The capital city of a country is usually a very important city. The government offices are located in the capital city and political leaders usually live there or nearby. There are many different types of governments in the world. The capital may also be the center of culture. There are often museums, libraries, and universities in the capital. Finally, the capital city can serve as a center of trade, industry, and commerce, so it is often the financial center of the country.

4.   The Japanese automobile industry uses robots in many stages of its production process. In fact, there is more than one robot for every ten production workers. Some Japanese universities are developing medical robots to detect certain kinds of cancer. Robots are used in Japanese automobile factories to perform dangerous tasks such as welding parts together. Soon super robots will be used for complicated tasks that are now done by human workers.

5.   The packaging of many products is very wasteful. Often the packaging is twice as big as the product. Packaging is used to protect things that are breakable. Many food items, for example, have several layers of extra packaging. Most of these extra layers could be eliminated.

Concluding Sentences

Some paragraphs end with a concluding sentence. This sentence states the main idea of the paragraph again using different words. It summarizes the main points of the paragraph, or makes a final comment on the topic. Concluding sentences are not always necessary. In fact, short paragraphs or paragraphs that are part of longer pieces of writing often do not have concluding sentences.

WRITING CONCLUDING SENTENCES

Write a concluding sentence for each paragraph.

1.   There are many reasons why I like wearing a uniform to school. First of all, it saves time. I don't have to spend time picking out my clothes every morning. Wearing a uniform also saves money. It's cheaper to purchase a few uniforms than to go out and buy lots of school clothes. In addition, I don't have the pressure of keeping up with the latest styles. Most importantly, wearing a school uniform gives me a sense that I belong. I really think it adds to the feeling of school spirit and community.

_____

_____.

2.   There are many reasons why I am against wearing my school uniform. For one thing, I don't like the style of the uniform. The navy blazer and plaid skirt are too conservative for me. Secondly, the uniform isn't comfortable. I prefer to wear baggy pants and a sweater instead of a skirt and jacket. Finally, I want the freedom to express my individuality through my style of dressing.

_____

_____.

3.   Credit cards have a lot of advantages. First of all, credit cards are convenient because you don't have to carry a lot of cash around. You can buy the products and services you need even if you do not have cash in your

pocket. In addition, credit cards are very helpful in emergencies. Finally, you can become a better money manager as you learn to use credit cards responsibly.

_____

_____.

CLASS ACTIVITY

A Your teacher will write this topic sentence on the board.

It is difficult to learn a new language.

B What details can you and your classmates think of to support this topic sentence? As you think of ideas, your teacher will write them in list form on the board. (Remember, these are just ideas, so they don't have to be complete sentences or in correct order.) Copy the list here.

_____   _____

_____   _____

_____   _____

C Discuss the list with your classmates. Cross out details that don't belong.

D With your classmates and teacher, choose the relevant ideas from the list above. Write them in sentence form on the board. Copy the sentences below.

_____

_____

_____

_____

_____

E With your classmates and teacher, organize the sentences and put them in correct paragraph form. Your teacher will write the paragraph on the board. Copy the finished paragraph below.

_____

_____

_____

_____

_____

A Choose one of the following topic sentences to write about. Make a list of supporting details. You do not have to write the list in complete sentences.

- Exercise is necessary for good health.
- Eating in restaurants is expensive.
- It is important for parents to teach their children about _____.
- _____ is a great place to visit.

Topic sentence: _____

Supporting details:

_____   _____

_____   _____

_____   _____

B Cross out any irrelevant details.

C Write the items on your list in complete sentences.

_____

_____

_____

_____

D Write a paragraph based on your list.

_____

_____

_____

_____

_____

Write a paragraph about one of the following topics.

- my proudest moment
- my job
- my worst day
- my favorite kind of music
- babies
- my _____

1. Write a topic sentence.

2. Make a list of supporting details.

3. Think about the ideas on your list. Cross out any idea that does not support your topic sentence.

4. Write your list in complete sentences.

5. Use the topic and supporting sentences to write a paragraph.

CHAPTER 3

Organizing Information by Time

In Chapter 1, you learned that organization is the key to good writing. There are several ways to organize sentences in a paragraph. Three of the most common ways are time order, order of importance, and space order. In this chapter you will practice organizing ideas by time.

Time Order

When you tell a story, you organize the events in the story by time. You tell what happened first at the beginning of the story. Then you tell what happened second, third, and so on. In writing, you often do the same thing.

Look at the pictures on page 23. They tell a story, but they are not in the right time order. Number the pictures so they tell the story in a logical time order. Then write a sentence or two about each picture.

1. _____

_____

2. _____

_____

3. _____

_____

4. _____

_____

IDENTIFYING TIME ORDER

When you write a paragraph, you will often have to organize events according to time. Read the model paragraph and answer the questions.

My Day

I had a terrible day yesterday. First, I woke up an hour late because my alarm clock didn't go off. Then, I was in such a hurry that I burned my hand when I was making breakfast. After breakfast, I got dressed so quickly that I forgot to put on socks. Next, I ran out of the house trying to get the 9:30 bus, but of course I missed it. Finally, I walked the three miles to my school only to discover that it was Sunday! I hope I never have a day as bad as the one I had yesterday.

1. What is the topic sentence?

_____

2. How are the supporting sentences organized?

_____

3. What is the concluding sentence?

_____

USING SIGNAL WORDS

In order to show time relationships, you will need to use signal words to guide the reader from one idea to the next idea. When you write a paragraph using time order, you will need to use the following signal words. Draw a circle around each signal word in the model paragraph *My Day*.

first	**next**	**as**
second	**before**	**later**
then	**after**	**finally**

USING PREPOSITIONS OF TIME

It is important to use correct prepositions to show time relationships.

A **Study the prepositions of time and the examples.**

Use *at* with specific times:	*at* 5:00 / *at* 7:30 / *at* noon / *at* midnight
Use *from* and *to* with a span of time:	*from* 6:00 *to* 9:00 / *from* 1941 *to* 1945
Use *in* with other parts of the day:	*in* the afternoon / *in* the morning / *in* the evening (exception: *at* night)
Use *in* with months:	*in* August / *in* June
Use *in* with years:	*in* 1999 / *in* 2001
Use *in* with seasons:	*in* the spring / *in* the summer / *in* the winter
Use *on* with days of the week:	*on* Sunday / *on* Tuesday / *on* Friday
Use *on* with specific dates:	*on* June 30 / *on* April 21, 2006 / *on* New Year's Eve

B **Complete the sentences with the correct prepositions.**

1. I lived in Madrid _____ 2000 _____ 2004.

2. Carmen was born _____ 1990.

(continued on next page)

3. She was born _____ October 31, _____ 4:00 _____ the afternoon.

4. I'll meet you for lunch _____ Tuesday _____ noon.

5. Ruth goes to New York every weekend. She takes the train _____ Saturday _____ 9:00 _____ the morning and arrives in New York _____ 10:45.

ORGANIZING SENTENCES BY TIME

Read the topic sentence. Then read the sentences below it. Together they tell a story. The sentences are not in the correct order. Number them so they follow a logical time order. Put a *1* in front of the sentence that should come first, and so on. Then use all the sentences to write the paragraph.

1. José saved his money and spent two months traveling around the world.

_____ He spent a week in New York and then flew to London and enjoyed several weeks in Europe.

_____ When he had seen the sights in Europe, José took a train to Istanbul and visited many places in Asia.

__*1*__ First, he flew from his home in Mexico City to New York City.

_____ After traveling through Asia, he went to South America and finally back home to Mexico.

_____

_____

_____

_____

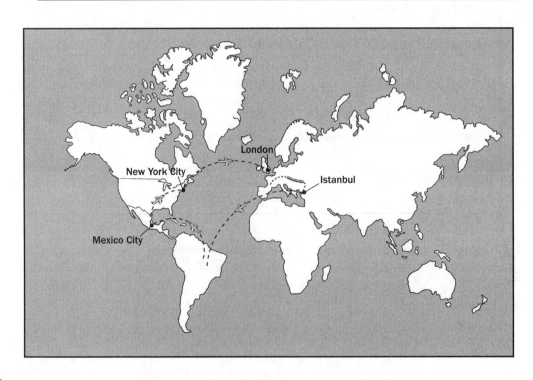

2. Tina had a hard time keeping her New Year's resolutions.

_____ As the months went on, she broke even more resolutions.

_____ On January 1, she wrote a list of New Year's resolutions.

_____ At the end of January, Tina had broken half of the resolutions.

_____ When the year ended, she realized that she had not kept a single resolution.

_____

_____

_____

_____

3. Mark decided that he wanted to plant a vegetable garden.

_____ At the end of the summer, he picked the vegetables from the garden.

_____ First, he went to a garden store and bought seeds.

_____ Then he went home, prepared the soil, and planted the seeds.

_____ Every day, Mark watered and weeded the garden.

_____

_____

_____

_____

WRITING PARAGRAPHS USING TIME ORDER

Write a paragraph about each of the following topics. Remember to begin with a topic sentence. Use signal words to guide the reader.

1. Vicki is having a birthday dinner for her friend. She made a list of things she has to do before the party. She put the things on her list in time order. Use her list to write a paragraph about the things she has to do.

buy food for dinner at supermarket

pick up birthday cake at bakery

clean house

make dinner

wrap present

set table

(continued on next page)

_____

_____

_____

_____

_____

2. Dr. Alden is the director of an English language school. Study her schedule for Tuesday, February 21.

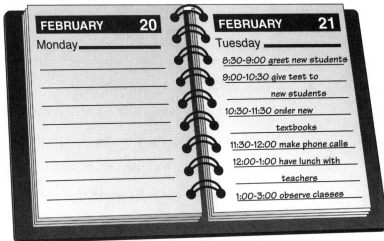

FEBRUARY **20**
Monday _____
_____
_____
_____
_____
_____
_____
_____

FEBRUARY **21**
Tuesday _____
8:30-9:00 greet new students
9:00-10:30 give test to
    new students
10:30-11:30 order new
    textbooks
11:30-12:00 make phone calls
12:00-1:00 have lunch with
    teachers
1:00-3:00 observe classes

_____

_____

_____

_____

_____

3. Babe Ruth was a famous American baseball player. The following time line gives you information about his life. Use the time line to write a paragraph about his life.

February 6, 1895:   born in Baltimore, Maryland

1914:   joined the Boston Red Sox

1920:   began to play for the New York Yankees

1921–34:   led the Yankees to seven championships

1936:   elected to the Baseball Hall of Fame

_____

_____

_____

_____

_____

_____

4. Elizabeth Blackwell was the first female medical doctor in the United States. The following time line gives you information about her life. Use the time line to write a paragraph about her life.

February 3, 1821:	born in Bristol, England
1832:	emigrated to New York City
1849:	graduated from Geneva Medical School in Geneva, New York
1853:	opened a dispensary in New York City because, as a woman, she could not get a job in a hospital
1868:	opened the Women's Medical College of the New York Infirmary
1875:	appointed professor at the London School of Medicine for Women
1910:	died in Hastings, England

_____

_____

_____

_____

_____

_____

_____

_____

_____

_____

CAPITALIZATION

Read this report about the history of the computer. All capital letters have been omitted. Correct the paragraph by putting capital letters in the proper places. You will need to add eighteen capital letters. Remember these rules of capitalization:

- Use a capital letter for names of people, titles, countries, states, cities, towns, streets, universities, days of the week, months of the year, and holidays.

- Begin the first word of every sentence with a capital letter.

- Begin the first word of a direct quotation (what someone says) with a capital letter.

- Capitalize the names of books, magazines, and movies.

throughout history, people have found it necessary to do mathematical computations and keep accounts. in early times, we used groups of sticks or stones to help make calculations. then the abacus was developed in china. these simple methods represent the beginnings of data processing. as computational needs became more complicated, we developed more advanced technologies. one example is the first simple adding machine that blaise pascal developed in france in 1642. another example is the first machine that would do calculations and print out results, which charles babbage designed in england in the 1830s. in the middle of the twentieth century, researchers at the university of pennsylvania built the first successful electronic computer. today, of course, we have the computer to perform all kinds of advanced mathematical computations.

On Your Own

Choose a famous person who interests you. Find information about his or her life. Make a time line based on the information and write a paragraph.

CHAPTER 4

Organizing Information by Order of Importance

In Chapter 3, you learned how to organize information according to time order. In this chapter you will learn how to put information in order according to its importance.

Order of Importance

It is often necessary to organize information according to order of importance. You can put the most important piece of information first, or you can save it for last.

RECOGNIZING ORDER OF IMPORTANCE

Read the following model paragraph and answer the questions.

> There are several ways to learn a new language. One way is to spend a lot of time watching television and listening to the radio. Another way is to take classes at a language school or university. The best way to learn a new language is to talk to native speakers.

1. What is the topic sentence?

_____

2. What three ways to learn a new language does the author mention?

_____

3. What does the author feel is the best way?

_____

USING SIGNAL WORDS

Remember to use signal words to guide the reader from one idea to the next idea.

A Study the list of signal words and phrases for paragraphs using order of importance.

first	second	moreover
first of all	third	most importantly
for one thing	also	for example
one reason that	in addition	finally
the next + *noun*	another + *noun*	the most important + *noun*
best / worst of all		

B Read the model paragraph and underline the signal words.

Bad drivers have several annoying habits. First of all, they change lanes often and don't use their turn signals. In addition, they are rude to other drivers. They get too close to the car in front of them, and they honk their horns. Worst of all, bad drivers ignore the speed limit and drive as fast or slow as they want.

ORDERING IDEAS ACCORDING TO IMPORTANCE

A In pairs or small groups, discuss this topic: the qualities of a good teacher. Then decide which supporting point is the most important. Put a *1* in front of that point. Decide the next most important point and put a *2* in front of it, and so on.

1. Qualities of a good teacher:

_____ has knowledge of subject

_____ cares about students

_____ has ability to explain clearly

Use the list to complete the paragraph that follows. The topic sentence has been given, but remember to include signal words.

A good teacher has several important qualities. _____

_____

_____

_____

Follow the same steps for the next two topics.

2. Things to consider when choosing a university:

_____ cost _____ quality of education

_____ location _____ size

There are four important things to consider when choosing a university. _____

_____

_____

_____

(continued on next page)

3. Advantages of marriage:

_____ having children

_____ having companionship

_____ sharing money

_____ working and making decisions together

Marriage has many advantages. _____

_____

_____

_____

_____

B **For the next three paragraphs, write your own topic sentence.**

1. Difficult things about living in a foreign country:

_____ new language

_____ unfamiliar customs

_____ different money

_____ feeling homesick

_____

_____

_____

_____

_____

2. Benefits of a higher education:

_____ have more employment opportunities

_____ earn higher salary

_____ gain prestige

_____ learn valuable information

_____

_____

_____

_____

_____

3. Ways to keep in good shape:

_____ eat well-balanced meals

_____ drink lots of water

_____ exercise daily

_____ get enough sleep

_____

_____

_____

_____

_____

WRITING PARAGRAPHS USING ORDER OF IMPORTANCE

A **Choose one of the following topics to write about.**

- things to consider when renting an apartment or buying a house

- advantages of learning a foreign language

- qualities of a good restaurant (or hotel, parent, politician, etc.)

- qualities of a bad restaurant (or hotel, parent, politician, etc.)

B **Make a list of supporting details on the lines provided. Do not worry about the order.**

_____ _____

_____ _____

_____ _____

C **Go over your list and cross out any items that do not belong. Then number the supporting ideas in order of their importance. Put a _1_ in front of the idea you feel is the most important, and so on.**

D **Write a topic sentence for your paragraph.**

_____

E **Using the topic sentence and your list of supporting points, write a paragraph about your topic on the next page. You may begin with what you feel is the most important point or save it for last. Remember to use signal words.**

_____

_____

_____

_____

_____

_____

F Remember that it is very hard to write a perfect paragraph on the first try. Read over your paragraph and look for ways to improve it. Use these questions to help you revise the paragraph you wrote. Rewrite your paragraph.

- Is there a topic sentence?

- Do all the sentences support the topic sentence?

- Are the sentences organized according to order of importance?

- Are there any irrelevant sentences?

- Did you include signal words to guide the reader from one idea to the next?

SMALL GROUP ACTIVITY

A In small groups, make a list of the advantages of living in a city.

_____   _____

_____   _____

_____   _____

_____   _____

B Write a paragraph based on your list. Organize your ideas according to the order of their importance. Save the biggest advantage for last.

_____

_____

_____

_____

_____

_____

C Follow the same procedure with the disadvantages of living in the city.

Equal Order Paragraphs

Sometimes you may feel that all of the points you are using as support are equally important. In this case, you list your points one by one. The order that you use is your choice.

Read the model paragraph. Notice that the author gives equal weight to each point.

> There are several things you can do to protect yourself when it gets very hot outside. First of all, you should avoid strenuous activity or wait until the sun goes down. In addition, it is a good idea to wear lightweight and light-colored clothing. It is also important to eat less food and drink more liquids. Finally, try to stay in air-conditioned buildings or go to the beach or the mountains.

1. What is the topic sentence?

_____

2. How many points does the author discuss? _____

WRITING PARAGRAPHS USING EQUAL ORDER

A Choose one of the following topics to write about.

- tips for staying healthy
- ways to do well in school
- things I like to do on the weekend

B Make a list of supporting details on the lines provided. Do not worry about the order.

_____   _____

_____   _____

_____   _____

C Go over your list and cross out any items that do not belong.

D Write a topic sentence for your paragraph.

_____

E Using the topic sentence and your list of supporting points, write a paragraph about your topic. You may put your supporting details in any order you choose. Remember to use signal words.

_____

_____

_____

_____

_____

_____

You Be the Editor

Read the following paragraph. It contains seven mistakes. Find the mistakes and correct them. Then rewrite the corrected paragraph.

Erik enjoy many types of sports. He is liking team sport such as basketball, soccer, and baseball. He also plays traditionals individual sports like racquetball and golf his favorite sports involve danger as well as exciting. He loves extreme skiing and skydiving.

On Your Own

Choose one of the other suggested topics from this chapter and write a paragraph about it.

CHAPTER 5

Organizing Information by Space

In this chapter you will learn how to organize information in a paragraph by space order.

Using Space Order

When you describe a place, you use space order to explain where things are located. The easiest way to do this is to choose a starting point. Then you describe where things are located in relation to your starting point. Decide on a logical method to follow. For example, when describing a room, choose a starting point and move clockwise around the room. Other methods are left to right, top to bottom, and back to front.

Read the model paragraph. Choose the picture of the room on page 39 that the paragraph describes. Circle that picture.

My bedroom is a special place. Like most rooms, it is a rectangle. When you walk in the door, the first thing you notice is the large window on the back wall. It has a beautiful view of the garden. My antique bed is under the window. The left wall is lined with bookcases where I keep my books and pictures. My dresser is on the wall to the right. There is a picture of my parents on the wall above the dresser. In the middle of the room, there is a handmade rug my parents bought in Mexico.

WRITING TOPIC SENTENCES FOR SPACE ORDER PARAGRAPHS

Write topic sentences for the following paragraphs.

EXAMPLE

The top of my desk is very well organized. My laptop computer is in the center where it is easy for me to reach. To the left of the computer, I keep a basket with pens, pencils, erasers, and paper clips. My calendar is right next to the basket. There is a small desk lamp in the right corner and a picture of my family next to it. It's very easy for me to work at my desk because everything is always in its place.

1. _____

In the center of the desk is a pile of old magazines and newspapers. The pile is growing every day. Next to that, there are several unwashed cups and a can of juice. There is a lamp in the left corner, but I use it to hold some baseball caps. An old box is on the right side of the desk. Inside the box are my letters and postcards. I also put CDs and DVDs in the box. The box is getting so full that soon I won't be able to put the top on it.

2. _____

There are beautiful roses along the fence in front of my house between the street and the driveway. I always put geraniums in my window boxes and pansies under the windows. I also keep a garden behind my house. I have irises, daisies, lilies, and other flowers planted there with a pretty brick path along the edge. I don't have much space left to plant new flowers!

3. _____

When you walk in the main entrance, the American art is on the first floor on your left. The Asian collection is directly in front of you and the Islamic art is on your right. European paintings and sculptures are on the left side of the museum on the second floor. The Egyptian mummies and statues are on the opposite side of the museum on the second floor. The Greek and Roman statues are on the left side of the third floor. Finally, the African collection is on the right side. It is a big museum with many famous works of art from all over the world.

USING SIGNAL WORDS

The signal words in space order paragraphs are often prepositions of place. Study the following list.

at	in	next to	on the right
at the end	in back of	on	on top of
behind	in front of	on both sides	over
beside	in the center	on the end	under
between	in the middle	on the left	

PRACTICING SPACE ORDER

A Look at the floor plan of the first floor of Lourie's Department Store. Then read the model paragraph that follows. It is organized by space order. Underline the signal words.

The first floor of Lourie's sells clothing and accessories for women and girls. As you enter the store through the main entrance, the jewelry department is directly in front of you in the middle of the store. The coat department is on the left and the cosmetics department is on the right. The junior shop is on the left, behind coats. Women's shoes are located in the left corner. Next to the shoe department, behind jewelry, is the sportswear department. Handbags and belts are next to sportswear in the right corner. The young girls' department is on the right, between handbags and cosmetics. The elevators are on the right wall.

B **Look at the picture of the jewelry department and complete the following sentences with the correct prepositions.**

1. The customers are standing _____ the counter.

2. The jewelry is _____ the case.

3. The little girl is standing _____ her parents.

4. The saleswoman is _____ the counter.

5. There is a mirror _____ the counter.

6. The sale sign is _____ the saleswoman.

WRITING PARAGRAPHS USING SPACE ORDER

A Complete the floor plan of the second floor of Lourie's using the information in the sentences.

Main Entrance

1. The elevators are on the wall on the right.
2. The men's casual clothing department is in front of the elevators.
3. The coat and suit department is in the middle of the second floor.
4. Men's shoes are to the left of the coat and suit department.
5. Swimwear for men is to the left of the entrance.
6. The shirt and tie department is in the left corner, behind the shoe department.

B Now write a paragraph describing the second floor. Use space order to organize the information. Begin with a topic sentence and use signal words.

The second floor of Lourie's has all the clothing a man needs. _____

_____

_____

_____

_____

_____

_____

C Write a paragraph describing the third floor based on the following floor plan. Use space order to organize the information. Begin with a topic sentence and use signal words.

(continued on next page)

_____

_____

_____

_____

_____

_____

_____

WRITING ABOUT A PLACE

A Choose one of the following places to write about. Then draw a picture of it in the box below. Make a list of some words you need in order to describe things in the space, such as furniture, windows, and clothes.

- your favorite room in your house or apartment
- your closet
- your favorite place to study
- your computer workstation or classroom

_____ _____

_____ _____

_____ _____

B Write a paragraph describing the place. Use space order to organize your
information.

_____

_____

_____

_____

_____

_____

C Ask one of your classmates to read your paragraph and draw a picture of
the place based on your description.

D Compare your picture and your partner's picture of the place. Are there
any differences? If yes, discuss them with your partner. Can you think of
ways to make your description clearer?

You Be the Editor

**Read the following paragraph. It contains eight mistakes. Find the mistakes
and correct them. Then rewrite the corrected paragraph.**

Our garage is use as a storage area. At the back of garage, there
are two bigs trash bins filled with old newspapers and magazines. to
be recycled. Against the right wall is an old workbench covered with
tool, bricks, and wood. On the opposite wall, we storing an old TV, a
folding cot, a fan, and my sisters tricycle. Its no surprise that our car is
parked in the driveway.

Choose one of the following topics and write a paragraph about it. Use space order to organize your information.

- a doctor's office
- a basic hotel room
- a flower garden
- the view out your window
- your school cafeteria

_____

_____

_____

_____

_____

_____

_____

Following the Writing Process

By now you probably understand that writing is a process that involves several steps.

Step One: Prewriting
thinking about your topic and organizing your ideas

Step Two: Writing
using your ideas to write a first draft

Step Three: Revising
improving what you have written

If you follow the steps, and practice by writing often, you will find it easier to write paragraphs and to improve your writing.

Step One: Prewriting

Prewriting is the thinking, talking, reading, and writing you do about your topic before you write a first draft. Prewriting is a way of warming up your brain before you write, just as you warm up your body before you exercise. Two helpful ways to warm up before you write are brainstorming and clustering.

BRAINSTORMING

Brainstorming is a quick way to generate a lot of ideas on a subject. The purpose is to make a list of as many ideas as possible without worrying about how you will use them. Your list can include words, phrases, sentences, or even questions.

To brainstorm, follow these steps:

1. Begin with a broad topic.
2. Write down as many ideas about the topic as you can in five minutes.
3. Add more items to your list by answering the questions *what, how, when, where, why,* and *who.*
4. Group similar items on the list together.
5. Cross out items that do not belong.

You can brainstorm ideas by yourself or with a group of people. You already did some brainstorming with your classmates in Chapter 2, when you made a list of ideas about the topic "It is difficult to learn a new language."

BRAINSTORMING ACTIVITY

A **Choose one of the following topics to brainstorm:**

- My best friend
- The importance of education
- Good manners
- Money brings _____

B **Write the topic at the top of a piece of paper and follow the steps for brainstorming.**

CLUSTERING

Clustering is another prewriting technique. It is a visual way of showing how your ideas are connected using circles and lines. When you cluster, you draw a diagram of your ideas.

To cluster, follow these steps:

1. Write your topic in the center of a blank piece of paper and draw a circle around it.
2. Write any ideas that come into your mind about the topic in circles around the main circle.
3. Connect these ideas to the center word with a line.
4. Think about each of your new ideas, write more related ideas in circles near the new ideas, and then connect them.
5. Repeat this process until you run out of ideas.

Look at the example of a cluster diagram on the topic of television commercials.

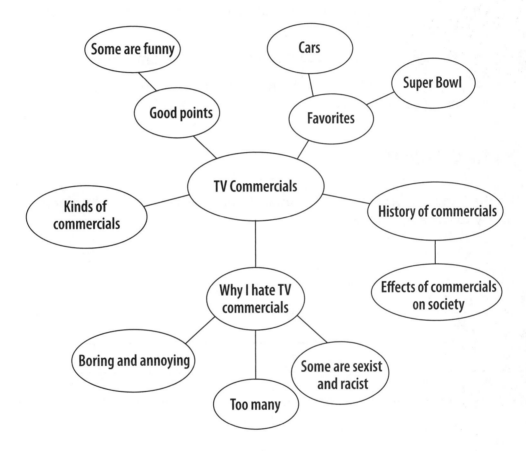

CLUSTERING ACTIVITY

On a separate piece of paper, practice clustering for a paragraph on one of the following topics:

- sports
- music
- after-school activities
- pets

Step Two: Writing

After you have spent some time thinking about your topic and doing the necessary prewriting, you are ready for the next step in the writing process: writing your paragraph. When you write the first draft of your paragraph, use the ideas you generated from prewriting as a guide.

As you write, remember to:

- Begin with a topic sentence that states the main idea.

- Include several sentences that support the main idea.

- Stick to the topic—do not include information that does not directly support the main idea.

- Arrange the sentences so that the order of ideas makes sense.

- Use signal words to help the reader understand how the ideas in your paragraph are connected.

WRITING ACTIVITY

Use the ideas you generated in the brainstorming activity or the clustering activity to write a paragraph.

_____

_____

_____

_____

_____

_____

_____

Step Three: Revising

It is almost impossible to write a perfect paragraph on the first try. The first try is called the first draft. After you complete the first draft, you must look for ways to improve it. This step is called revising. When you revise your paragraph, you can do the following:

- Add new ideas to support the topic.

- Cross out sentences that do not support the topic.

- Change the order of the sentences.

Use the following checklist to revise your paragraphs.

Revising Checklist

☐ Make sure you have a topic sentence.

☐ Cross out sentences that do not relate to the main idea.

☐ Check to see if the sentences are in the right order.

☐ Add new ideas if they support the topic sentence.

☐ Make sure you have included signal words to help guide the reader.

☐ Check the punctuation, spelling, and grammar.

REVISING ACTIVITY

Read the paragraph. Think about ways to improve it. Use the revising checklist above to help you. Revise the paragraph and then rewrite it.

My cat Rufus has several annoying habits. For one thing, he likes to hop on my lap when I'm trying to read. He must think that my computer mouse is a toy to play with. His most annoying habit is jumping on the table when we're having dinner. He knows that he can't have any table food. Another problem is that Rufus enjoys scratching the furniture. He's smart and will hide in the cellar when it's time for his medicine.

_____

_____

_____

_____

_____

Now find a place in the paragraph to add this sentence.

Rufus sometimes chases birds up a tree and then can't get down.

PRACTICING THE STEPS OF THE WRITING PROCESS

A Read the situation and write a paragraph using the steps of the writing process.

Your friend is having trouble learning English. You are writing him/her a note of encouragement. You want to give some tips about how to learn English.

PREWRITING

B Brainstorm a list (or make a cluster diagram) of ideas about how to learn English.

WRITING

C Write a paragraph that gives advice about how to learn English. Use the information from your prewriting as a guide. Remember to begin with a good topic sentence and to organize your sentences in a logical order.

_____

_____

_____

_____

_____

_____

_____

REVISING

D Read over your paragraph. Think about ways to improve it. Use the revising checklist on page 51 to help you. Revise your paragraph and then rewrite it.

_____

_____

_____

_____

_____

_____

_____

A Read the situation and write an article. Complete the steps of the writing process with a partner.

You are writing an article about international students for your local newspaper. You want to include a paragraph about one of your classmates.

PREWRITING

B Make a list of questions that you want to ask your partner.

Here are some suggestions:

- Where are you from?
- What is your native language?
- Have you visited any other countries? What are they?
- Do you know any other languages?
- Why are you learning English?

You might also want to ask questions about your classmate's:

- family
- hobbies
- interests
- career or career plans
- education
- travel experiences

C Talk to your partner and ask him or her the questions you wrote. Write the answers on a piece of paper.

WRITING

D Write the paragraph of the article that describes the person you interviewed. Use the information from your questions as a guide. Remember to begin with a good topic sentence and to group similar ideas about your classmate together.

_____

_____

_____

_____

_____

_____

_____

E Now ask your partner to read your paragraph. Does he or she have any suggestions? Write down your partner's suggestions. You can also use the revising checklist on page 51 to help you. Revise your paragraph and then rewrite it.

On Your Own

Choose one of the topics on pages 48 and 49 that you did not already write about. Write a paragraph on the topic. Practice the steps of prewriting (brainstorming or clustering), writing, and revising. Remember to use the revising checklist on page 51.

CHAPTER 7

Supporting the Main Idea

The Main Idea

You have learned that a paragraph has one main idea that is supported with details. Supporting details can come from many places, such as your own personal experience, examples, quotations, or facts.

Using Personal Experience

Writing about a personal experience is one way of supporting a topic sentence. Read the following model paragraph and answer the questions.

> Sometimes a stranger can be a real friend. The woman who helped me in the library yesterday is a great example. I needed to find some books for a report, but I didn't know how to use the computer in the library. She saw me looking at the computer screen and asked if I wanted her help. She showed me how I could find a book by its title, author, or subject by following the instructions on the screen. She then helped me print out the information. The woman even showed me how the books in the library are organized so that I could find what I needed easily. After I thanked her, she said she wanted to help me because all students should know how to use the library.

1. What is the topic sentence?

_____

2. How are the supporting sentences organized?

_____

WRITING ABOUT PERSONAL EXPERIENCES

PREWRITING

A Discuss these expressions with your classmates. What do they mean?

- Money is the root of all evil.

- Two heads are better than one.

- Variety is the spice of life.

- Haste makes waste.

- Don't count your chickens before they hatch.

WRITING

B Choose one expression to write about. Use an experience from your own life to prove or disprove the expression.

_____

_____

_____

_____

_____

_____

REVISING

C Read over the paragraph you wrote. Look for ways to improve it. Use the revising checklist on page 51 to help you. Revise and then rewrite your paragraph.

INDIVIDUAL ACTIVITY

PREWRITING

A Use a personal experience to write a paragraph that supports one of the expressions below. Before you write the paragraph, brainstorm a list of ideas.

- Good things happen when you least expect them.

- Sometimes hard work is not rewarded.

- Things often don't turn out the way you planned.

_____   _____

_____   _____

_____   _____

_____   _____

WRITING

B Now use your list to write the paragraph supporting the expression you chose.

_____

_____

_____

_____

_____

REVISING

C Read over the paragraph you wrote. Look for ways to improve it. Use the revising checklist on page 51 to help you. Revise and then rewrite your paragraph.

Using Facts and Statistics for Support

Good writers often use facts, statistics, or statements from experts to support their topic.

READ AND RESPOND

Read the article. Underline the facts and statistics that support the main idea.

The Planet in 2050

The population of the world will experience many changes by 2050. According to Joel E. Cohen, professor of population at Columbia University, the worldwide population will rise to 9.1 billion from the current 6.5 billion. However, the rate of population growth will actually slow. For the first time, there will be more people living in cities than in rural areas. In addition, the proportion of people living in developing countries will increase. Less developed regions had twice the population of developed countries in 1950. That rate will be greater than six to one by 2050. Still another change will be the balance between young and old people. Before 2000 there were more young people than old people on earth. By 2050, one person in three living in developed countries will be sixty years or older.

1. What is the main idea of this article?

_____

2. What facts and statistics are used to support the main idea?

_____

_____

_____

WRITING ABOUT INFORMATION IN GRAPHS AND CHARTS

Facts and statistics are often presented in graphs and charts. Sometimes you will need to interpret the information in a graph, chart, or table and use it as support. Here are some words that will help you.

increase	rise	less / fewer
decrease	fall	percent
remain the same	same	percentage

Student Enrollment

PREWRITING

A Look at the graph below and answer the questions that follow. The name of the graph tells you what kind of information is presented.

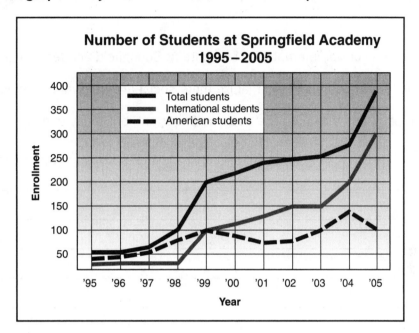

Number of Students at Springfield Academy 1995–2005

1. In what year was the number of international students equal to the number of American students? _____

2. In 1999, how many international students attended Springfield Academy?

   _____

3. In 2004, how many American students attended Springfield Academy?

   _____

4. In what year did the number of American students remain the same as the year before?

   _____

5. In what years did the number of international students remain the same as the year before?

   _____

6. When did enrollment of international students go over 100?

   _____

7. In what year were there twice as many international students as American students?

   _____

WRITING

B You are an international student at Springfield Academy, and you feel that there should be more social and cultural activities for international students. Since the number of international students is growing every year, you believe that the school has a responsibility to help them socially and culturally as well as academically. Use specific information from the graph to write the part of the paragraph that describes the student body.

Since the number of international students at Springfield Academy is growing every year, the school needs to organize more social and cultural activities for us. In the past, this may not have been so important, but today things are different. In 1995, _____

_____

_____

_____

_____

_____

_____

Because international students now represent such a large percentage of the student body, I believe that the school has a responsibility to help us outside the classroom. For example, I would like the school to organize sightseeing tours and arrange visits with American families.

REVISING

C Read over your part of the paragraph and look for ways to improve it. Use the revising checklist on page 51 to help you. Revise your part of the paragraph and then rewrite it.

International Student Majors

A There will be a new English language school. You have been asked to write a report describing the programs that should be offered at the school. Look at the chart below and answer the questions. The name of the chart tells you what kind of information is presented.

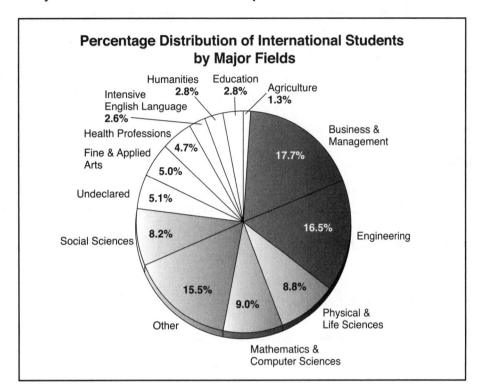

Percentage Distribution of International Students by Major Fields

Humanities 2.8%
Education 2.8%
Agriculture 1.3%
Intensive English Language 2.6%
Health Professions 4.7%
Fine & Applied Arts 5.0%
Undeclared 5.1%
Social Sciences 8.2%
Other 15.5%
Mathematics & Computer Sciences 9.0%
Physical & Life Sciences 8.8%
Engineering 16.5%
Business & Management 17.7%

1. What is the most popular field? _____

2. What percentage of all international students in the United States are studying engineering?

   _____

3. What is the second most popular field? _____

4. What percentage are studying business and management? _____

5. This means that almost _____ percent of all international students are studying either engineering or business and management.

6. This is followed by _____ percent studying mathematics and computer sciences and _____ percent studying social sciences.

7. What are some other fields that international students study? _____

   _____

WRITING

B Based on information in the chart, you feel that the school should have a lot of courses in technical English. Complete the paragraph from the report. Support the topic sentence with facts from the chart.

There is a growing need to provide more technical English programs to

international students. _____

_____

_____

_____

_____

REVISING

C Read over your paragraph and look for ways to improve it. Use the revising checklist on page 51 to help you. Revise your paragraph and then rewrite it.

The Facts about Running

PREWRITING

A Study the graph and answer the questions.

1. What is the name of the graph?

_____

2. When does the runner achieve the greatest decrease in the amount of time it takes to run five miles (eight kilometers)? _____

3. How long does it take a typical runner to run five miles (eight kilometers) at the end of the first year? _____

4. How long does it take at the end of the second year? _____

5. What happens during the following five years? _____

_____

6. How long does it take during the seventh year? _____

7. How many minutes does the amount of time decrease during the first seven-year period?

_____

WRITING

B You are writing a letter to new members of your running club. Many of the new members are discouraged because it is taking them so long to run five miles. You want to encourage them to continue running. Complete the letter. Support the main idea with facts from the graph.

Dear Members,

   I know that some of you are discouraged because it is taking you so long to

run five miles. But don't give up yet. _____

_____

_____

_____

_____

_____

_____

REVISING

C Read over your paragraph and look for ways to improve it. Use the revising checklist on page 51 to help you. Revise your paragraph and then rewrite it.

Using Quotations for Support

A quotation from an expert on your topic can make your paragraph stronger. Be sure to punctuate the quotations correctly.

RULES FOR PUNCTUATING QUOTATIONS

When you quote someone, follow these rules:

- Put the speaker's exact words inside quotation marks.

- Put a comma after the words that introduce the speaker's words.

- Put periods, commas, or question marks inside the final quotation mark.

EXAMPLE

The doctor said, "Call me if you don't feel better by Monday."

A **Read the paragraphs and the quotations that follow. Notice that the quotations can be used to support the ideas in the paragraph. Rewrite the paragraphs on a separate piece of paper, adding the quotations where they belong.**

1.

Energy Prices and Conservation Rise

The cost of energy is high and continues to rise. People across the country are feeling the effects of the rising costs. As a result, many people are trying to conserve energy at home. They are turning off lights and electrical appliances when they are not using them. People are also trying to use less heat in the winter and use their air conditioners less frequently in the summer. In addition, some Americans are trying to conserve energy on the road. They are buying smaller cars that use less gas. Many also use public transportation or carpool to save gas. High prices will continue to force people to look for ways to cut back.

---

a. "Heating a home with natural gas could cost an average of about $1,200 this winter, up from $1,000 last year, according to projections by the department's Energy Information Administration. The cost for homes using heating oil is expected to increase to about $1,480 from $1,220 last year. Electricity and propane prices are rising, too." (Eileen Alt Powell, business writer)

b. "Set your thermostats at 75 degrees in the summer and 68 degrees in the winter. This way you will be comfortable and save money and energy." (Gerald Christopher, director of the Energy Conservation Center)

2.

Cell Phones and Safety

Talking on a cell phone and driving do not mix. Unfortunately, too many people are combining the two activities and the results could be deadly. The National Highway Traffic Safety Administration (NHTSA) reports that 54 percent of drivers have a cell phone in their car and 73 percent have used their phone while driving. The number of drivers using cell phones during daytime hours increased from 6 percent in 2002 to 8 percent (more than a million drivers) in 2004. The biggest jump was in young drivers ages 16 to 24. People who talk on the phone and drive often become distracted and do not pay enough attention to driving. Distraction can cause accidents that result in serious injury and death. One study from the University of Utah found that even hands-free cell phones are a distraction. Motorists were 18 percent slower in braking and took 17 percent longer to regain speed after braking. Motorists need to be educated about safe cell-phone use.

---

a. "To drive safely, a driver needs to give priority attention to the driving task. Even a momentary distraction can lead to a crash." (L. Robert Shelton, Executive Director of NHTSA)

b. "There are multiple distractions in the car and while driving—cell phones should not be one of them. No call is worth a life." (Tom Wheeler, CEO of Cellular Telecommunications and Internet Association)

3.

Volcanoes and Climate

Volcanic eruptions influence climate by cooling the earth's atmosphere. After the Indonesian volcano Krakatoa erupted in 1883, the surface temperature of the earth was cooler for several years. Eruptions create large clouds of volcanic dust around the earth. Less of the sun's energy can reach the earth. Gases from the eruption rise high into the atmosphere and collect the sun's radiation. To understand how volcanoes change climate, scientists study the long-term effects of powerful volcanic eruptions. For example, they study Mount Katmai in Alaska, which erupted in 1912.

---

a. "There are twenty-two volcanoes around the globe sending tons of sulphur dioxide into the atmosphere. The sulphur dioxide just sits there and blocks sunlight." (Reid Bryson)

b. "Studying such events will help scientists be better prepared for the next major eruption and give them clues about changes to expect." (Luke Oman)

You Be the Editor

Read the following article about diet guidelines. It contains eight mistakes. Find the mistakes and correct them. Then rewrite the corrected article.

New Guidelines for Diets   3234

In 2005 the government announced new guidelines to help people loose weight. Tommy Thompson, the Secretary of Health and human Services, said, "Nearly two-thirds of American are overweight or obese, and more than 50 percent of us do not get the recommended amount physical activity." Extra weight and lack of exercise can raise the risk of cancer, diabetes, heart disease, and stroke. The guidelines emphasizes healthier eating and physical activity. People are advise to eat more fruits, vegetables, and whole grains. and to choose poultry, fish, and meats without a lot of fat. They are encouraged to get at least thirty minutes of exercise every day. Each person need to make the right food and exercise choices.

On Your Own

1. Look through newspapers and magazines for a chart or graph that interests you. Make a copy or cut it out of the newspaper or magazine. Write a paragraph explaining the information in the chart or graph.

2. With a partner, make up your own information for a chart or graph on a topic of interest to you. Then write a paragraph interpreting the data.

CHAPTER 8

Giving Instructions

When you explain the step-by-step process of how to do or make something, you are giving instructions. In this chapter you will learn how to write instructions that are clear and easy to follow. When you write instructions or directions, you need to use time order, and sometimes space order.

Recognizing Processes

Read the following model paragraph and answer the questions.

How to Pack a Suitcase

Most people hate to pack, but following these steps helps make packing easy. First, put all the items you want to take on your bed and organize everything into groups. For example, put all your shoes in one group, all your clothes in another, all your toiletries in a third, and so on. Second, put your toiletries in plastic bags and your shoes in shoe bags. After that, place your shoes on the bottom of the suitcase. Then take your pants, skirts, or dresses, fold them in half, and roll them up. Once rolled, place them in the bottom of the suitcase around the shoes. Fill empty space on the bottom with socks and underwear. Next, fold and put flat items, such as shirts, blouses, and sweaters, as a second layer. Put your bags of toiletries between layers of clothes. Finally, place your last layer of items in the suitcase so that there are no spaces left between items. This way of packing helps you get organized and stay organized when you travel.

1. What is the topic sentence?

_____

2. What steps does the author give?

_____   _____

_____   _____

_____   _____

3. How are the steps organized?

_____

WRITING TOPIC SENTENCES FOR PROCESS PARAGRAPHS

The topic sentence of a process paragraph must identify the process and tell something about it. Write a topic sentence for the following paragraphs.

There are several steps you must follow to get a library card at your neighborhood library.

First, ask for an application at the librarian's desk or at the book check-out counter. Write your name and address on the form. Then, present identification such as a report card or a student identification card that shows your age or grade level. Wait for your application to be processed and your library card to be mailed. Finally, sign your library card and put it in a safe place.

1. _____

_____.

First of all, write your name and address in the upper left-hand corner of the envelope. Then write the name and address of the person you are mailing the letter to in the center of the envelope. This usually takes three lines. Put the name on the first line. Write the street address on the second line and the city and state on the third line. Remember to include the zip code. Finally, put a stamp in the upper right-hand corner. The most important thing to remember is to write neatly!

2. _____

_____.

First, fill a clean vase with water. Second, cut most of the flowers and greens so they are approximately two times the height of your vase. Then, cut a couple of the flowers two inches longer. After you are finished cutting the flowers, you can begin to put the greens in the vase. Now add the flowers. Start at the outer edge of your vase. Put the longest flowers in the center of your arrangement. Then take a few steps back and admire your bouquet.

3. _____

_____.

Hold the toothbrush at an angle so that the brush points toward your gums. To clean the outside of your front teeth, use a back-and-forth motion or brush in small circles. Then, brush the outside back teeth. Make sure to brush each tooth. To clean the inside of your teeth, hold the toothbrush at an angle and use short strokes. Now, hold the brush flat and scrub gently across the biting surfaces of your teeth. Finally, give your tongue a few brushstrokes to remove bacteria.

USING SIGNAL WORDS

When you describe a process you put the steps in time order. In order to make the steps clear, you should use time order signal words to guide the reader from one step to the next. Review the signal words on page 25. Complete the following paragraph about how to make popcorn. Use the correct signal words.

It is very easy to make good popcorn. _____*First*_____ , put three

tablespoons of oil in a large heavy pot. _____ , heat the

oil on a high flame until one kernel of popcorn pops when you drop it

into the hot oil. When the oil is hot enough, pour one-quarter cup of

popcorn into the pot and cover it with a lid. _____ ,

reduce the flame to medium and begin to shake the pot gently.

Continue shaking the pot until all the corn has popped.

_____ , empty the popcorn into a large bowl and add

melted butter and salt.

RECOGNIZING THE ORDER OF INSTRUCTIONS

Making Fruit Cups

A The following sentences describe how to make a dessert that uses fresh fruit, but the sentences are not in the correct time order. Find the topic sentence and put a *1* in front of it. Use the signal words to help you put the steps in the right order.

_____ Then, put the melon in the refrigerator to chill.

_____ Finally, top each fruit cup with sherbet.

_____ Fruit cups are easy to make.

_____ Begin by cutting one or more melons in half and removing the seeds.

_____ Next, combine several types of fruits such as sliced peaches, oranges, and bananas, and chill in the refrigerator.

_____ Before serving, fill the melon halves with the chilled fruit.

B Now write the ordered steps in paragraph form.

_____

_____

_____

_____

_____

_____

_____

_____

The Heimlich Maneuver

A The following sentences describe what to do if someone is choking. First, find the topic sentence. Then put the sentences in the right order.

_____ Then make a fist with one hand and grasp the fist with your other hand. Put your hands just below his or her rib cage.

_____ The Heimlich maneuver is a method that anyone can use to help someone who is choking on a piece of food.

_____ Finally, press your fist into the victim's abdomen with a quick upward movement.

_____ The first thing you should do is stand behind the choking person and put your arms around his or her waist.

_____ If the person is still choking, you may need to repeat the maneuver.

B Now write a paragraph based on the steps.

_____

_____

_____

_____

_____

_____

_____

_____

_____

_____

Potting a Plant

A Study the pictures. They show how to pot a plant. Use the pictures to number the steps that follow in the correct time order.

_____ make a hole in center of soil

_____ press soil down with thumbs

_1_ cover bottom of pot with small stones

_____ drop plant into soil

_____ put two inches of soil on top of stones

_____ water plant

_____ add more soil until it almost reaches top of pot

B Now read the following topic sentence and complete the paragraph about how to pot a plant.

It is easy to pot a plant if you follow the right procedure. _____

_____

_____

_____

_____

_____

_____

_____

Writing a Process Paragraph

Choose one of the following processes to write about.

How to:

- plan a party
- make your favorite dish
- change a flat tire on a bicycle
- study for an exam
- make your bed
- plant a garden

PREWRITING

A Make a list of all the steps in the process.

_____   _____

_____   _____

_____   _____

B Number the steps so they are in the correct time order.

WRITING

C Write a paragraph describing the process. Use the list of steps from your prewriting as a guide. Be sure to write a topic sentence that clearly states the process that you are describing.

_____

_____

_____

_____

_____

_____

_____

_____

_____

REVISING

D Read over your paragraph and look for ways to improve it. Use the revising checklist on page 51 to help you. Revise your paragraph and then rewrite it.

DESCRIBING THE STEPS IN AN EXPERIMENT

Processes are very important in scientific and technical fields.

A **Study the following lab report.**

WATER EXPANSION EXPERIMENT	
Purpose: To show that water expands when frozen	
Materials: A glass jar	
Procedure:	
1. Fill the glass jar halfway with water.	
2. Mark the outside of the jar at water level.	
3. Put the jar in the freezer until the water freezes.	
4. Observe the new water level.	
Results: The level of the frozen water is higher.	

B **Now read the following model paragraph that describes the process of the experiment. Then answer the questions.**

You can do a simple experiment to prove that water expands when it is frozen. All you need is an empty glass jar. First, fill half the jar with water. Then mark the water level on the outside of the jar. After that, put the jar in a freezer until the water freezes. When the water is frozen, take the jar out of the freezer and observe the new water level. You will see that the level of the frozen water is higher. This proves that water expands when it is frozen.

1. What is the topic sentence? _____

_____

2. What signal words are used in the paragraph? _____

_____

3. How many steps are described? _____

WRITING ABOUT AN EXPERIMENT

PREWRITING

A Read the following lab report. Discuss it with a classmate.

SOLAR ENERGY EXPERIMENT
Purpose: To show that black is a better collector of solar energy than white
Materials: 2 tin cans, black and white paint, room thermometer
Procedure:
1. Paint the cans—one black, one white.
2. Fill the cans with water.
3. Put the cans in direct sunlight for three hours.
4. Check the temperature of the water in the cans and compare.
Results: The water in the black can is hotter.

WRITING

B Now use the information to write a paragraph describing the process of the experiment. Remember to begin with a topic sentence and use signal words.

_____

_____

_____

_____

_____

_____

_____

REVISING

C Read over your paragraph and look for ways to improve it. Use the revising checklist on page 51 to help you. Revise your paragraph and then rewrite it.

USING TIME ORDER AND SPACE ORDER TO GIVE DIRECTIONS

When you explain to someone how to get to a specific place, you are giving directions. In order to make your directions clear, you need to use both time order and space order.

A Study this list of useful words for writing directions.

continue	between _____ and _____
go as far as _____	in the middle
go north (or south, east, west)	next door to
go one block (or two blocks, etc.)	on the corner
go past _____	on the left (or the right)
go straight (until you come to _____)	on the left side (or the
turn left (or right)	right side)
across the street from _____	

B Look carefully at the map of the historical area of Philadelphia. Find the Visitor Center on the map. Where is it located?

_____

C Read these model directions.

In order to get from the Visitor Center to the U.S. Mint, follow these directions. First, go north two blocks from the Visitor Center. Then turn left on Arch Street. Continue two blocks on Arch Street to 5th Street. Turn right on 5th Street. The U.S. Mint is on your right.

D You work at the Visitor Center. Write directions from the Visitor Center to each of the following places for a tour guidebook.

1. Liberty Bell Pavilion

_____

_____

_____

_____

_____

2. Free Quaker Meeting House

_____

_____

_____

_____

_____

3. First Bank of the United States

_____

_____

_____

_____

_____

4. Franklin Court

_____

_____

_____

_____

_____

(continued on next page)

5. Graff House

_____

_____

_____

_____

_____

You Be the Editor

Read the following paragraph. It contains nine mistakes. Find the errors and correct them. Then rewrite the corrected paragraph.

To remove a tick and avoid infections, follow these step. First, use fine-point tweezers to get hold of tick as close to the skin as you can. Then, gently pull the ticks out without squeezing it's body. After that, place the tick in a small container. So that it can be tested by a lab or a veterinarian. Next, wash you hands and clean the site of the bite and the tweezer with disinfectant. Finally, watch for signs for illness and call your doctor to find out if you needed treatment.

On Your Own

1. Draw a simple map of your neighborhood. Label the streets and important buildings. Practice the vocabulary of giving directions by writing directions from your house to several other places. Check your directions by having another student follow them.

2. Write a paragraph that tells how to protect yourself when a hurricane, blizzard, tornado, or other natural disaster is forecast for your area.

3. Write a paragraph that describes the steps involved in getting your driver's license.

CHAPTER 9

Writing Descriptions

Writing a description is like creating a picture using words. The key to writing a good description is using specific details that create exactly the picture you want.

Describing People

Read the model paragraph and answer the question that follows.

The police are looking for a woman who stole a diamond necklace from Dayton's Jewelry Store. According to the store manager, the woman is approximately five feet tall, very thin, light-skinned, and about sixty years old. She has short, straight gray hair and wears glasses. Her most distinguishing mark is the dimple in her chin. When she was last seen, she was wearing heavy blue eye make-up and large, silver hoop earrings. She had on a short black coat and black pants. If you see anyone fitting this description, contact the police department immediately.

What details does the author use to describe the woman?

_____   _____

_____   _____

_____   _____

USING DESCRIPTIVE WORDS

When you write a description you should use words that relate to the senses of sight, sound, touch, smell, and taste. These are called sensory words. Sensory words help the reader imagine what you are describing.

WORDS FOR DESCRIBING PEOPLE

When you describe what a person looks like, you write about physical characteristics such as height, weight, and hair color. Again, the key to writing a good description is to use details that help the reader imagine the person you are describing. Here are some words that can help you describe people.

Height	Body Type	Hair	Features
medium	athletic	blonde	beard
short	heavy	brunette	dimple
tall	muscular	curly	freckles
	petite	dark	glasses
	plump	light	mole
	skinny	long	mustache
	stocky	red	scar
	thin	short	wrinkles
		straight	
		wavy	

WRITING A DESCRIPTION OF A PERSON

Read this telephone conversation.

Lucia: I'm so glad you called. I have a big problem and I hope you can help me.

Kim: What's the problem? I'll help if I can.

Lucia: My friend has tickets to the All-Star Music Concert and I'm supposed to pick them up at the community center at seven o'clock. The problem is that I just found out I have to babysit because my mother is working late. Can you possibly pick up the tickets for me?

Kim: Sure. How will I recognize your friend?

Lucia: Well, he's medium height and average weight. He wears glasses, and he usually carries an MP–3 player.

Kim: That description could fit a lot of guys. Can you be more specific?

Lucia: Well, his hair is dark and curly. Sometimes he wears a baseball cap.

Kim: What's his name?

Lucia: Angelo Sinclair.

Kim: OK, no problem. I'll find him.

Lucia: Thank you so much!

A At the last minute, Kim is unable to go to the community center. Her brother Lee agrees to meet Angelo instead. Kim is writing a note to Lee describing Angelo so he will be able to find him. What should Kim's note say? Make a list of ideas. The following questions will help you.

- Is he tall or short?

- Is he fat or thin?

- What color hair does he have?

- Is his hair curly or straight?

- Does he wear glasses?

- Is there anything about him that you notice immediately?

WRITING

B Pretend you are Kim. Write a note to Lee describing Angelo.

Dear Lee,

_____

_____

_____

_____

_____

REVISING

C Read over your note and make sure you have added enough details. Revise your note and then rewrite it.

INDIVIDUAL ACTIVITY

PREWRITING

A Choose a member of your family or a friend to describe. Make a list of descriptive details.

_____   _____

_____   _____

_____   _____

WRITING

B Using your list as a guide, write a description of your relative or friend. Remember to include descriptive words from page 81.

_____

_____

_____

_____

_____

_____

_____

REVISING

C Read over your description and make sure you have a topic sentence and enough descriptive detail. You can also use the revising checklist on page 51 to help you. Revise your description and then rewrite it.

CLASS ACTIVITY

A Choose someone in your class to describe.

B Write a short description of that person, but do not mention his or her name. Remember to include details about size, hair color, distinguishing marks, and so on. Write your description on a separate piece of paper.

C Give the description to your teacher. The teacher will give each student one of the descriptions. Read the description you were given. Can you guess who it is?

On Your Own

Write a description of one of the boys in this picture. You might need to review some vocabulary with your teacher.

Describing Objects

When you describe things, or objects, you want to create a picture with words.

WORDS FOR DESCRIBING OBJECTS

Here are some words you can use to describe objects.

Color	Texture	Size	Smell	Taste	Shape
black	rough	average	fresh	bitter	oval
orange	sharp	big	fruity	bland	rectangular
purple	silky	huge	pungent	fruity	round
yellow	smooth	small	smokey	nutty	square
			strong	salty	
				sour	
				spicy	
				sweet	

Read the model paragraph and answer the question that follows.

I found the perfect backpack to give my sister for her twelfth birthday. The backpack has wide, padded shoulder straps to distribute weight evenly. The back is padded, and the pack has a strap that goes around the waist. There are pockets for books and all her school supplies: writing paper, folders, pencils, crayons, erasers, and markers. The backpack even has room for a laptop computer. The pack has wheels so it can be rolled. The best thing about the backpack is that it is lightweight and won't be too heavy when it is filled with books.

What details does the author use to describe the backpack?

_____   _____

_____   _____

_____   _____

_____   _____

DESCRIBING PRODUCTS

A You work in the advertising division of Lourie's Department Store. You are working on the holiday mail-order catalog. You have just completed the first page. Reread your product descriptions.

1. Keep warm this winter with this practical but good-looking plaid blanket. It is 52 inches (132 cm) wide and 76 inches (193 cm) long, with fringe on two sides. It is handmade in England of the finest-quality wool. $100. Item A31.

2. Everyone can enjoy a fun ride with this lightweight and strong scooter. It can hold up to 200 pounds of weight. A smooth ride is guaranteed. The scooter has a rear fender brake for easy stopping. It folds easily for storing. $60. Item D12.

3. You'll love this cashmere sweater. It has long sleeves, and five pearl buttons down the front. It comes in four colors: black, white, red, and blue. It is available in sizes small, medium, and large. $99. Item A17.

4. This beautiful, antique Chinese vase makes a perfect gift. It is 18 inches (46 cm) tall and comes with a wooden stand. It has two handles and is available in blue or white. $200. Item B5.

B Now write short descriptions of these items for the next page of the catalog. Use your imagination. Remember, when you describe an object, you will need to mention such things as shape, size, color, and texture.

1.

2.

3.

1. _____

_____

2. _____

_____

3. _____

_____

WRITING A DESCRIPTION OF A BUILDING

PREWRITING

A Draw a picture of a special building in your hometown. Then make a list of important details about the building.

_____   _____

_____   _____

_____   _____

B Write a description of the building. Use your prewriting list as a guide.

_____

_____

_____

_____

_____

C Give your description to a classmate and ask him or her to draw the building using your description.

REVISING

D Compare the picture your classmate drew to your description. How are they alike? What are the differences? The differences should give you clues to help you revise your paragraph. Revise your paragraph and then rewrite it.

Describing Places

A Read the following postcard that Carolyn wrote to her friend Sharon.

Hi,

    I'm sorry I didn't get to see you while you were in Boston. It was so hot here that we went to our favorite campsite in the mountains. The site is very clean and rarely crowded. It's near the top of Mount Greylock in the Berkshires. The trails are long and shady. From the tower at the top of the mountain you can look at the valleys and rivers below. The view is spectacular in the evening. The sky turns bright orange and pink as the sun sets behind the hills. Best of all, there's always a nice cool breeze! Let me know when you'll be in Boston again.

                    Love, Carolyn

Sharon Laroche
84 Maple Street
Hawthorne, NY 10532

What details does the author use to describe Mount Greylock?

B Read the list of words that can be used to describe places.

clean	hilly	old
cold	hot	quiet
colorful	humid	rural
cool	industrial	sandy
crowded	modern	spectacular
dirty	mountainous	wide
flat	narrow	windy

C Pretend you are on vacation on a beach. Write a postcard to a friend describing it. Use at least nine descriptive words. Underline the descriptive words you use.

PAIR ACTIVITY

In this activity you will write a description of the hometown of one of your classmates. If everyone is from the same place, ask your partner questions about another city he or she has visited. Follow these steps.

PREWRITING

A Talk to your partner about his or her hometown. First, make a list of questions to ask your partner.

Here are some suggestions:

● What is the name of your hometown?

● Where is it located?

- What size is it?

- How many people live there?

- What is the weather like?

- What is the most impressive thing about your hometown?

You might also want to ask questions about:

- history

- geography

- architecture

- services

- entertainment

- famous people who have lived there

B Copy your questions on a separate piece of paper. Leave enough space to write in your partner's answers. Ask your partner the questions you prepared.

WRITING

C Use the information you have about your partner's hometown to write a paragraph. Be sure to give the name of the place in the topic sentence.

_____

_____

_____

_____

_____

_____

REVISING

D Now ask your partner to read your paragraph. Does he or she have any suggestions? Revise your paragraph based on your partner's suggestions. You can also use the revising checklist on page 51 to help you. Revise your paragraph and then rewrite it.

INDIVIDUAL ACTIVITY

Think about your favorite place to go and relax. Is it a beach? Your bedroom? A coffee shop?

PREWRITING

A Brainstorm a list of details describing the place.

_____   _____

_____   _____

_____   _____

WRITING

B Use your list to write a paragraph.

_____

_____

_____

_____

_____

_____

REVISING

C Read over your description. Did you include enough specific details about the place? What else can you include to make your description clearer? Use the revising checklist on page 51 to help you. Revise your paragraph and then rewrite it.

You Be the Editor

Read the following description of a missing dog. It contains six mistakes. Find the mistakes and correct them. Then rewrite the corrected paragraph.

My dog, Bette, is missing. She is a small black poodle with browns eyes. her hair is short and curly. Bette weighs eight pounds and is about one and a half foots long. She has a short tail, long, floppy ears, and small feet. She is wear a silver collar with an ID tag on it. She is very friendly around people and love children. I have had Bette for six years, since she was a puppy, and I miss her very much. I am offering a $50 reward for anyone which finds Bette. Please call me at 305-555-7671.

REWARD!
$50
For the Return of Lost Pet

NAME: BETTE
AGE: 6 YEARS
SEX: FEMALE
WEIGHT: 8 POUNDS
COLOR: BLACK
COLLAR: SILVER
　　　　　WITH ID TAG

CALL: 305-555-7671

On Your Own

Imagine you are one of the *paparazzi*—photographers who follow famous people and take their pictures. You have just taken a good photo of a famous person and you contact a magazine to try to sell your photo. Name the person and describe the photograph. What does he or she look like in the picture? What is he or she wearing? What other things or people are in the picture? (If you cannot imagine a photo, look for one in a magazine or newspaper and describe it.)

EXAMPLE

I have a photograph of Prince William. He is walking on a London street. He is wearing sunglasses and a gray raincoat. He has a new hairstyle, and he is holding hands with a beautiful lady. She looks much older than the prince! They are both carrying small shopping bags with the name of a famous jeweler on them.

CHAPTER 10

Expressing an Opinion

Opinion

When you write, it is often necessary to state your opinion about something you believe to be true.

Read the article below and the two opinion paragraphs. Answer the questions that follow each paragraph.

The number of children in public schools in the United States who speak little or no English is increasing rapidly. A recent study shows that 18 percent of children in the United States speak a language other than English at home. The number of children who have little skill in English grew by nearly a million between 1994 and 2000. More than fifty languages other than English have been identified in the schools of California. The number of children who are English learners will continue to grow in the future. These students and their teachers face many challenges, including what language to use in the classroom. Some people believe children of immigrants should be taught in their native language. Others believe that these children should be taught in English only.

1.   In my opinion, children of immigrants should be taught in their native language. First of all, these children will feel more comfortable in a strange school if they hear and speak their native language. In addition, they will be able to understand subjects like math, history, and science more easily if they are taught in their native language and do not have to struggle with the new language. Finally, students who use their native language in school are better able to keep their cultural identity.

a. What is the author's opinion?

_____

_____

b. What three reasons does the author give to support his or her opinion?

_____

_____

_____

2.   In my opinion, children of immigrants should be taught in English. First, they will learn the new language more quickly if all their subjects are taught in English. Second, children of immigrants will feel less isolated if they are taught in the same language as the rest of the children. Finally, they will be able to perform better on standardized tests if they have learned the material in their classes in English.

a. What is the author's opinion?

_____

_____

(continued on next page)

b. What three reasons does the author give to support his or her opinion?

_____

_____

_____

STATING YOUR OPINION

Read the following sentences. Circle the word or phrase in parentheses that you think best expresses your opinion.

> EXAMPLE
>
> It is _____ for mothers with small children to work outside of the house. (**good** / **harmful**)

1. Community service _____ be a requirement for graduation. (**should** / **should not**)

2. Nuclear energy _____ the best way to meet our energy needs. (**is** / **is not**)

3. Women _____ be required to serve in the army. (**should** / **should not**)

4. Prayer _____ be allowed in the public schools. (**should** / **should not**)

5. It _____ acceptable to use animals for laboratory experiments. (**is** / **is not**)

6. Photo identification _____ be required of all voters. (**should** / **should not**)

7. Governments _____ use the death penalty to punish criminals. (**should** / **should not**)

8. _____ is the most exciting sport. (**Hockey** / **Soccer** / **Tennis**)

9. Modern architecture _____ ugly. (**is** / **is not**)

10. UFOs (unidentified flying objects) _____ exist. (**do** / **do not**)

WRITING TOPIC SENTENCES THAT STATE YOUR OPINION

The following useful phrases are often used to introduce opinions that serve as topic sentences.

I believe (that)	I think (that)
In my opinion,	I feel (that)

Write an opinion topic sentence for each of the statements in the previous activity.

In my opinion, it is good for mothers with small children to

work outside of the house.

1. _____

2. _____

3. _____

4. _____

5. _____

6. _____

7. _____

8. _____

9. _____

10. _____

SUPPORTING YOUR OPINION

In the body of the paragraph, you will give reasons, examples, or facts to support your opinion. It is helpful to list your reasons in order of importance. The following phrases are often used as signal words to introduce facts, reasons, and examples.

First of all,	In addition,	Secondly,
For one thing,	Moreover,	Thirdly,
One reason that	For example,	Finally,
Also,		

Choose three of your opinions and give two or three reasons, examples, or facts to support each one.

EXAMPLE

Opinion:	**In my opinion,** it is good for mothers with small children to work outside of the house.
Reason 1:	A working mother can help pay for the many things the children need.
Reason 2:	A working mother is a good role model for her children, especially her daughters.
Reason 3:	Children who have caregivers other than their mothers learn better social skills.

(continued on next page)

1. **Opinion:** _____

   Reason 1: _____

   Reason 2: _____

   Reason 3: _____

2. **Opinion:** _____

   Reason 1: _____

   Reason 2: _____

   Reason 3: _____

3. **Opinion:** _____

   Reason 1: _____

   Reason 2: _____

   Reason 3: _____

WRITING AN OPINION PARAGRAPH

PREWRITING

A Look at the opinions and reasons you wrote in the last exercise. Choose one of your opinions as the topic for a paragraph.

WRITING

B Write a paragraph. Use your opinion as the topic sentence. Then use your reasons to write supporting sentences. Remember to use signal words.

_____

_____

_____

_____

_____

_____

_____

REVISING

C Read over your paragraph and look for ways to improve it. Use the following questions to help you. Revise your paragraph and then rewrite it.

- Does the topic sentence state your opinion?

- Do you have two or three reasons to support your opinion?

- Have you used signal words to introduce your reasons?
- Are there any irrelevant sentences?

PAIR ACTIVITY

PREWRITING

A Discuss the following list of sentences about children and TV with a partner. Some of the sentences support the opinion that TV is good for children. Other sentences support the opinion that TV is bad for children.

1. TV exposes children to different countries, cultures, and ideas.
2. Children can learn about science, history, and the arts.
3. There is too much violence on TV.
4. Children see a false picture of human relationships.
5. Educational programs teach children basic skills such as reading and writing.
6. Watching TV is too passive. Children should be doing more creative and active things.
7. Children want to buy everything they see on commercials.
8. TV can be harmful to children's eyes.
9. News programs inform children about what is going on in their community.
10. TV gives children free and interesting entertainment.

B With your partner, divide the list into two groups.

TV Is Good for Children	TV Is Bad for Children
_____	_____
_____	_____
_____	_____
_____	_____
_____	_____
_____	_____
_____	_____

WRITING

C The principal of your school has asked you to write an article about children and television for the school newsletter. What is your opinion? Is TV good or bad for children? Choose an opinion with your partner, then use your opinion as the topic sentence for your paragraph. Use the list of reasons in B as supporting sentences. Add any other reasons you can think of to support your opinion.

_____

_____

_____

_____

_____

_____

_____

_____

REVISING

D Revise your paragraph on a separate piece of paper by adding two of the following sentences. Be sure to choose the ones that support your opinion and put them in a logical place. Revise your paragraph and then rewrite it.

- There are over seven acts of violence per hour on prime-time TV.

- The most violent TV shows are on Saturday mornings, when many children are watching.

- When children see something on TV, they become interested and want to learn more about it.

- Children learn to recognize famous people.

- News programs teach children about important things that are going on in the world.

PREWRITING

A Read the letter and answer the questions that follow.

Dear Editor:

Last month our nine-year-old daughter was hit by a car. The man driving the car was drunk at the time and didn't stop at a stop sign. Our little girl was in the hospital for three long weeks. My husband and I didn't know if she would live or die. It was a terrible time for us. Although today she is alive, we are afraid something like that might happen again.

Recently we heard that the punishment for the driver was only a $500 fine. He didn't go to jail and he didn't lose his license. Today he is free to drive and possibly commit the same crime again. Maybe next time he will kill somebody.

We feel the laws against drinking and driving should be very strict. Drunk drivers should pay for their crimes. We think their licenses should be taken away. We need stricter laws!

Yours truly,

Kathleen Johnson

Kathleen Johnson
Philadelphia, PA

1. Do you think drinking and driving is a serious crime? _____

2. Which of the following do you think is a fair punishment for drinking and driving? Why?

   _____ lose license   _____ lose car

   _____ get jail sentence   _____ pay fine of $500 or more

WRITING

B Write a paragraph that expresses your opinion about drinking and driving.

_____

_____

_____

_____

_____

_____

REVISING

C Read your paragraph again. Do all your sentences support your opinion? Are all your reasons clear? Revise your paragraph and then rewrite it. This time include one of the following facts:

- A National Highway Traffic Safety Administration report found that drinking by drivers caused more than 17,000 deaths in 2003.

- More than 40 percent of all traffic fatalities in the United States are caused by drunk drivers.

SMALL GROUP ACTIVITIES

Read and Respond

PREWRITING

A Read this news article and study the police report. In small groups, discuss the situation and the three suspects. Together, decide who you think committed the crime.

Computer Crime Hits Local Bank

NATIONAL CITY BANK and Trust Company is the largest bank in the city. Its assets are in the billions of dollars. In 1960 the bank computerized its operations. The bank had considered itself very lucky because it had not been troubled by computer crime—until last week. On Wednesday, the accountants discovered that a total of $400,000 was missing from several different accounts. It is not yet known where the funds were transferred. Police investigation has led to three possible suspects. These three people had easy access to the computer system that transferred the funds out of the bank.

POLICE REPORT

(a) Norman Glass—Computer operator
   –has worked for bank six months
   –earns low salary
   –has wife and four children
   –lives in large house and drives expensive new car
   –before working at bank he served five years in army (won a Medal of Honor)
(b) Alicia Santana—Vice president of bank
   –has been with bank 35 years
   –has a good history with bank
   –recently lost a lot of money in stock market
   –takes expensive vacations
   –earns very high salary
(c) Jim Tomlin—Computer consultant
   –has worked for bank two years
   –is active in church and community
   –graduated top of his class at Harvard
   –supports widowed mother who is sick and lives in expensive nursing home
   –has a gambling problem

WRITING

B Write a paragraph stating your opinion about who you think committed the crime. Be sure to give specific reasons to support your opinion.

_____

_____

_____

_____

_____

_____

_____

_____

REVISING

C Read over your paragraph and look for ways to improve it. Use the revising checklist on page 51 to help you. Revise your paragraph and then rewrite it.

Giving Advice

A If you were the advice consultant for your newspaper, how would you respond to the following letters? Respond to each one with your opinion. Then share your responses with your classmates.

1.

Dear Adviser:

My friend always borrows things and doesn't return them. Once he borrowed my favorite sweater to wear to a party. I had to ask him three times before I got it back. Last month he borrowed my tennis racket and still hasn't returned it. Yesterday he asked to borrow money, and I told him I was broke. What do you think I should do?

Arnie T.

Dear Arnie T.:

_____

_____

_____

_____

_____

_____

_____

The Adviser

2.

Dear Adviser:

My friend and I are having a terrible argument and we hope you can settle it for us. I say it's OK for girls to call boys on the telephone. I say it is all right for a girl to let a guy know she likes him and would like to go out with him. My friend disagrees. She says that guys still prefer to do the courting, but girls make it difficult now because they are so aggressive. She says guys still prefer the old-fashioned type of girl. Who do you think is right?

Confused

Dear Confused:

_____

_____

_____

_____

_____

_____

_____

_____

_____

The Adviser

B Exchange your paragraphs with a partner. Tell each other if you are convinced by the other person's opinions. Give each other advice on how to make your opinions stronger. Rewrite your response letters before you give them to your teacher.

You Be the Editor

Read the following letter. It contains eight mistakes. Find the mistakes and correct them. Then rewrite the corrected letter.

Dear Editor:

In my opinion, it is important for women with small childrens to work outside of the home. First of all, is to difficult to be with little kids all day. Womens needs a break from there kids. Also, a woman who has a career can offer her children mores. It is the quality of time that mothers spend with their children that are important.

Sincerely,

Lisa Harris

On Your Own

Write a paragraph giving your opinion on one of the following topics.

- curfews for students
- eating a vegetarian diet
- what society should do about crime
- allowing women to serve in the military

Comparing and Contrasting

Similarities and Differences

Very often in your writing you will need to show how things are similar or different. When you *compare* two things, you show how they are similar. When you *contrast* two things, you show how they are different.

A Study these two pictures. Look for similarities and differences.

B Make a list of the similarities and another list of the differences.

Similarities	Differences
_____	_____
_____	_____
_____	_____
_____	_____
_____	_____

Comparing

RECOGNIZING SIMILARITIES

A **Read the model paragraph.**

Ann and Beth are identical twins, so it's easy to understand the embarrassing mistake I made yesterday. I was planning to ask Ann for a date, but it turned out I asked Beth. The two sisters look exactly alike. Both girls are tall and thin with short curly brown hair. They also have the same unusual blue-green eye color. In addition, Ann wears gold-rimmed glasses and so does Beth. Finally, both Ann and Beth have freckles. I wouldn't be surprised if they even have the exact same number of freckles. Now I have to explain my mistake to both of them.

B **What characteristics about Ann and Beth does the paragraph compare?**

_____   _____

_____   _____

_____   _____

THE LANGUAGE OF COMPARISON

English uses special sentence patterns to make comparisons.

A **Study the following patterns of comparison using *and*.**

Affirmative sentences *with the verb* **be**

Ann is a student. Beth is a student.

a. Ann is a student <u>and</u> Beth *is* <u>too</u>.
b. Ann is a student <u>and</u> <u>so</u> *is* Beth.

Affirmative sentences *with other verbs*

Japan exports cars. Germany exports cars.

a. Japan exports cars and Germany *does* <u>too</u>.
b. Japan exports cars <u>and</u> <u>so</u> *does* Germany.

Negative sentences *with the verb* **be**

The blue dress isn't expensive. The green dress isn't expensive.

a. The blue dress isn't expensive, and the green dress *isn't,* <u>either</u>.
b. The blue dress isn't expensive, <u>and</u> <u>neither</u> *is* the green dress.

Negative sentences *with other verbs*

Owls don't sleep at night. Mice don't sleep at night.

a. Owls don't sleep at night, <u>and</u> mice *don't* <u>either</u>.
b. Owls don't sleep at night, <u>and</u> <u>neither</u> *do* mice.

Practice using these structures. Follow the example.

> EXAMPLE
>
> Ann runs four miles a day. Beth runs four miles a day.
>
> a. *Ann runs four miles a day and Beth does too.*
>
> b. *Ann runs four miles a day and so does Beth.*

1. Mark plays the piano. Jorge plays the piano.

    a. _____

    b. _____

2. The bank opens at 9:00 A.M. The grocery store opens at 9:00 A.M.

    a. _____

    b. _____

3. Yukio doesn't ski. Cristina doesn't ski.

    a. _____

    b. _____

4. Skiing is an exciting sport. Surfing is an exciting sport.

    a. _____

    b. _____

5. The Khans don't have a car. The Riveras don't have a car.

    a. _____

    b. _____

6. Tunis is an old city. Cairo is an old city.

    a. _____

    b. _____

7. Suzanne lives in a small apartment. Amanda lives in a small apartment.

a. _____

b. _____

8. Charlie isn't friendly. Liz isn't friendly.

a. _____

b. _____

9. Children need love. Adults need love.

a. _____

b. _____

B Now study these patterns of comparison.

● **the *same* + noun + *as***

Carla speaks the same <u>language</u> as José.
       (noun)

This book is the same <u>price</u> as that one.

My house is the same <u>color</u> as yours.

● ***as* + adjective/adverb + *as***

Sam is as <u>tall</u> as his father.
     (adjective)

Paula is as <u>serious</u> as Anita.

Women's clothes are as <u>expensive</u> as men's clothes.

Anton draws as <u>carefully</u> as Monica.
        (adverb)

Indira dresses as <u>well</u> as Stephanie.

Practice using these patterns. Follow the example.

> EXAMPLE
>
> Danny weighs 185 pounds. Arthur weighs 185 pounds.
>
> a. (noun: *weight*) *Danny is the same weight as Arthur.*
>
> b. (adjective: *heavy*) *Danny is as heavy as Arthur.*

(continued on next page)

1. Mary is five feet tall. John is five feet tall.

    a. (noun: *height*) _____

    b. (adjective: *tall*) _____

2. This car costs $18,500. That car costs $18,500.

    a. (noun: *price*)

    _____

    _____

    b. (adjective: *expensive*)

    _____

    _____

3. My house has eight rooms. Your house has eight rooms.

    a. (noun: *size*) _____

    b. (adjective: *big*) _____

4. Jeffrey was born in 1990. Omar was born in 1990.

    a. (noun: *age*) _____

    b. (adjective: *old*) _____

5. This story is seventy pages long. That story is seventy pages long.

    a. (noun: *length*) _____

    b. (adjective: *long*) _____

6. The teacher speaks loudly. The student speaks loudly.

    a. (noun: *voice*) _____

    b. (adverb: *loudly*) _____

SIGNAL WORDS OF COMPARISON

English uses many other special words and phrases to show comparison.

A **Study the following list.**

both	**similar**
have . . . in common	**similar to**
like	**the same**
similarly	**likewise**

B Read the following model paragraph and underline all the expressions of comparison.

  Scientific American and *Discover* are similar monthly magazines. First of all, they have several sections in common. For example, both magazines have articles about science, technology, and medicine. In addition, both have special departments, including letters from readers and reviews of current books about the sciences. Both cover some of the same scientific developments. Another similarity is that both magazines illustrate articles with colorful photographs, diagrams, charts, and graphs. Finally, both of these magazines cost $4.99, and both are widely read.

C Make a list of the similarities between the two magazines.

_____ _____

_____ _____

_____ _____

WRITING COMPARATIVE SENTENCES

A These sentences are based on the paragraph above. Combine the sentences using the words in parentheses. You may need to refer back to the paragraph.

> **EXAMPLE**
>
> *Scientific American* and *Discover* are both monthly magazines. (and so)
> *Scientific American is a monthly magazine and so is Discover.*

1. Both *Scientific American* and *Discover* are monthly magazines. (and so)

_____

2. *Scientific American* and *Discover* report on scientific developments. (and . . . too)

_____

3. Both magazines cost $4.99. (the same . . . as)

_____

(continued on next page)

4. *Scientific American* uses many illustrations and so does *Discover*. (both)

_____

5. Both magazines have special departments. (and . . . too)

_____

B Write a sentence of comparison for each of the following pairs of words. Use a variety of structures and vocabulary.

> EXAMPLE
>
> The Empire State Building / the Statue of Liberty
>
> *The Empire State Building is in New York City and so is the*
> *Statue of Liberty.*

1. England / United States

_____

2. Abraham Lincoln / John F. Kennedy

_____

3. lemons / bananas

_____

4. tennis / Ping-Pong

_____

5. chemistry / biology

_____

C Write four sentences comparing Jane Wexler and Ruth Friedman. Base your comparisons on the information provided on their driver licenses.

ALABAMA STATE
Department of Motor Vehicles
DRIVER LICENSE
Eye color: **Brown**
Hair color: **Black**
Height: **5'3"**
Date of Birth: **6/30/61**
Jane Wexler

ALABAMA STATE
Department of Motor Vehicles
DRIVER LICENSE
Eye color: **Brown**
Hair color: **Black**
Height: **5'3"**
Date of Birth: **6/30/61**
Ruth Friedman

1. _____

2. _____

3. _____

4. _____

D Study the following ads. Write four sentences of comparison based on your observations and the information provided.

Lourie's
Ladies' turtleneck
Machine washable
Cotton blend
Sizes 4-14
red, navy, white, green
$34.99

Green's
Ladies' turtleneck
Machine washable
Cotton blend
Sizes 4-14
red, navy, white, green
$34.99

1. _____

2. _____

3. _____

4. _____

WRITING TOPIC SENTENCES FOR COMPARISON PARAGRAPHS

When you write the topic sentence for a comparison paragraph, you must state the two things that you are comparing.

A Look at the following sample topic sentences.

Time and *Newsweek* are very similar weekly magazines.

Time and *Newsweek* have several things in common.

Time and *Newsweek* are alike in many ways.

Time and *Newsweek* share many similarities.

Time is similar to *Newsweek* in several ways.

B Write three different topic sentences for each of the following paragraphs.

1. _____. First of all, both cities are hot and humid most of the year. The typical daytime temperature in both places is about 92 degrees Fahrenheit (33 degrees Celsius) with humidity of 99 percent. It also rains a lot during the summer in Short Hills and White Plains. The evenings and nights are warm in both places.

   a. _____

   b. _____

   c. _____

(continued on next page)

2. _____. The main similarity is that both dogs are very friendly. Spot loves people, and so does Freckles. In addition, both of my dogs are smart and can do lots of tricks. For example, both can roll over on command. Another similarity is that both dogs are picky eaters. They only like the most expensive dog food.

a. _____

b. _____

c. _____

WRITING A PARAGRAPH OF COMPARISON

PREWRITING

A Study this biographical information about two important Americans, Benjamin Franklin and Thomas Jefferson.

BENJAMIN FRANKLIN

1706–1790

- founded University of Pennsylvania
- helped write Declaration of Independence
- important person in American Revolution
- well-known philosopher and thinker
- ambassador to France

THOMAS JEFFERSON

1743–1826

- author of Declaration of Independence
- third president of United States
- foreign Minister to France
- founded University of Virginia
- philosopher, architect, inventor
- played important role in American Revolution

B Make a list of the similarities between the two men.

_____   _____

_____   _____

_____   _____

_____ _____

_____ _____

WRITING

C Complete the paragraph comparing these two famous Americans. Use your list of similarities as a guide.

Benjamin Franklin and Thomas Jefferson have many things in common. _____

_____

_____

_____

_____

_____

_____

REVISING

D Read over your paragraph and look for ways to improve it. Use the revising checklist on page 51 to help you. Revise your paragraph and then rewrite it.

INDIVIDUAL ACTIVITY

PREWRITING

A Choose one of the following topics to compare.

- two similar movies you have seen
- two similar restaurants you have been to
- two similar teachers you have had
- two similar sports you enjoy
- two similar people you know

B Before you begin to write the first draft of your paragraph, make a list of similarities between the two things you are comparing. (Look back at the lists of words to describe people, places, and things in Chapter 9.)

_____ _____

_____ _____

_____ _____

C Now write a paragraph of comparison. Be sure to identify the two things you are comparing in the topic sentence. Then use the list of similarities from B as your guide.

_____

_____

_____

_____

_____

_____

REVISING

D Read over your paragraph and look for ways to improve it. Use the revising checklist on page 51 to help you. Revise your paragraph and then rewrite it.

Contrasting

When you describe the differences between two people, places, or things, you are contrasting them.

RECOGNIZING DIFFERENCES

A Read the following model paragraph.

> When Michael was in Sedona last week, he ate at two very different restaurants. He had lunch at Cantina Italiana and dinner at the Cityside Café. First of all, the food at Cantina was delicious, but unfortunately, the food at Cityside was terrible. The atmosphere at Cantina Italiana was much better than the one at Cityside. Cantina was clean and quiet; however, the Cityside Café was dirty and noisy. The server at the Cantina Italiana was much more polite than the server at Cityside. In fact the server at Cityside was quite rude. Finally, the meal at Cityside Café was much more expensive than the meal at Cantina. Michael will always remember his delicious lunch at Cantina Italiana, but he can't wait to forget his terrible dinner at Cityside Café.

B Make a list of the differences between the two restaurants.

Cantina Italiana	Cityside Café
_____	_____
_____	_____
_____	_____
_____	_____

THE LANGUAGE OF CONTRAST

Adjectives that are used to describe the differences between two people or things are called comparative adjectives.

A Read the model paragraph.

> Maya and Linda are sisters, but they are different in many ways. For one thing, their physical appearances are very different. Maya is taller and thinner than Linda. Linda has darker eyes and longer hair than Maya. Their personalities are also different. Maya is more serious and more ambitious than Linda. She is a better student because she studies harder than her sister. On the other hand, Linda is more creative and more social than Maya.

To form comparative adjectives, follow these rules:

- Add *-er* to one-syllable adjectives.

  hard ➤ harder

- For adjectives that end in *y*, change the *y* to *i* and add *-er*.

  busy ➤ busier

- Add *more* in front of longer adjectives.

  beautiful ➤ more beautiful

Note these common exceptions:

Adjectives		Comparative Adjectives
good, well	➔	better
bad	➔	worse
far	➔	farther, further

B Reread the model paragraph on page 117 and underline the comparative adjectives.

C Practice using comparative patterns. Follow the example.

> **EXAMPLE**
>
> Gary weighs 178 pounds. Gerald weighs 165 pounds.
>
> *Gary is heavier than Gerald.*

1. The Nile is more than 4,160 miles (6,695 kilometers) long. The Amazon is about 4,000 miles (6,437 kilometers) long.

_____

2. Mt. Everest is 29,035 feet (8,850 meters) high. Mt. Fuji is 12,388 feet (3,776 meters) high.

_____

3. The third chapter is very difficult. The fourth chapter isn't as difficult.

_____

4. Ann is a very careful driver. Paul isn't a very careful driver.

_____

SIGNAL WORDS OF CONTRAST

English uses many signal words to show contrast.

A Study the following list and example sentences.

Signal Words	Example Sentence
although	*Although* my mother is talkative, my father is quiet.
however	My mother is talkative. *However,* my father is quiet.
on the other hand	My mother is talkative. *On the other hand,* my father is quiet.
but	My mother is talkative, *but* my father is quiet.
yet	My mother is talkative, *yet* my father is quiet.
different from	My mother's personality *is different from* my father's personality.
unlike	*Unlike* my mother, my father is quiet.

B Underline the signal words that show contrast in the paragraph below.

The Reporter and Style magazines are very different weekly magazines. First of all, they have different sections. The Reporter has sections on politics, finance, science, and culture. On the other hand, Style has sections on fashion, home decorating, cooking, and gardening. In addition, The Reporter costs $3.50 per issue, but Style costs $5.00 per issue. Finally, The Reporter is translated into ten languages, but Style is only in English.

WRITING CONTRAST SENTENCES

Write a sentence of contrast for each of the following pairs of words.

> **EXAMPLE**
>
> feather / rock
>
> *A feather is lighter than a rock.*

1. Alaska / Florida

_____

2. airplane / train

_____

3. classical music / rock 'n' roll

_____

4. Volkswagen / Rolls Royce

_____

5. ice cream / rice

_____

WRITING TOPIC SENTENCES FOR CONTRAST PARAGRAPHS

When you write the topic sentence for a contrast paragraph you must state the two things that you are contrasting.

A **Look at the following list of sample topic sentences.**

The Reporter and *Style* are very different weekly magazines.

The Reporter and *Style* are different in many ways.

The Reporter and *Style* have many differences.

The Reporter and *Style* differ in several ways.

B **Write three different topic sentences for each of the following paragraphs.**

1. _____. First of all, the temperature in Westland is usually hotter than it is in Eastfalls. In Westland it is often in the nineties, but in Eastfalls, the temperature rarely goes above eighty. Secondly, the humidity is much higher in Westland than it is in Eastfalls. It rains a lot in Westland; however, it is usually dry in Eastfalls. Overall, the weather in Eastfalls is more pleasant.

a. _____

b. _____

c. _____

2. _____. For one thing, they are different in appearance. Fluffy is a small, curly-haired dog, but Shane is big and shaggy. Another difference is their personality. Fluffy is very friendly and loves people. On the other hand, Shane is shy and afraid of people. Finally, my two dogs differ in their intelligence. Unlike Shane, Fluffy is smart and can do lots of tricks.

a. _____

b. _____

c. _____

WRITING PARAGRAPHS OF CONTRAST

An Apartment

PREWRITING

A You and your family are looking for an apartment close to public transportation. You saw these two descriptions of apartments in the newspaper. Read the descriptions.

NEW AGE APTS—2 bedroom apt. with patio available immediately in large modern building. Short distance to bus stop. Unfurnished. Pets allowed. Only $950/month plus utilities.	Fairfax Apartments—large 3 bedroom apt. Only 2 blocks from train station. Air conditioned. Furnished. No pets. All utilities included. Available Sept. 1, $1,200/month.

B Now write five sentences of contrast about the two apartments.

1. _____

2. _____

3. _____

4. _____

5. _____

WRITING

C Which apartment would you choose? Write a paragraph explaining your decision and the differences between the two apartments.

_____

_____

_____

_____

_____

_____

REVISING

D Read over your paragraph and look for ways to improve it. Use the revising checklist on page 51 to help you. Revise your paragraph and then rewrite it.

A Trip to Hawaii

A You and a friend are planning a trip to Hawaii. You found these advertisements in the newspaper. Read the advertisements.

PLAN A

HAWAIIAN FLING

Price: **$1799**

Length: **8 DAYS, 7 NIGHTS**

Includes:
- welcome party
- deluxe hotel accommodations
- visit to two islands *(Oahu and Maui)*
- breakfast and dinner
- transportation to and from airport
- guided tours around each island

PLAN B

Spend the vacation of your dreams in

HAWAII

Price: $2899

Length: 15 days, 14 nights

Includes:
- welcome party
- deluxe hotel
- visit to two islands (Oahu and Maui)
- breakfast and dinner
- transportation to and from airport

B Make a list of differences between the two trips.

_____   _____

_____   _____

_____   _____

WRITING

C Write a one-paragraph e-mail message to your friend contrasting the two plans and suggesting the one you think would be better for you.

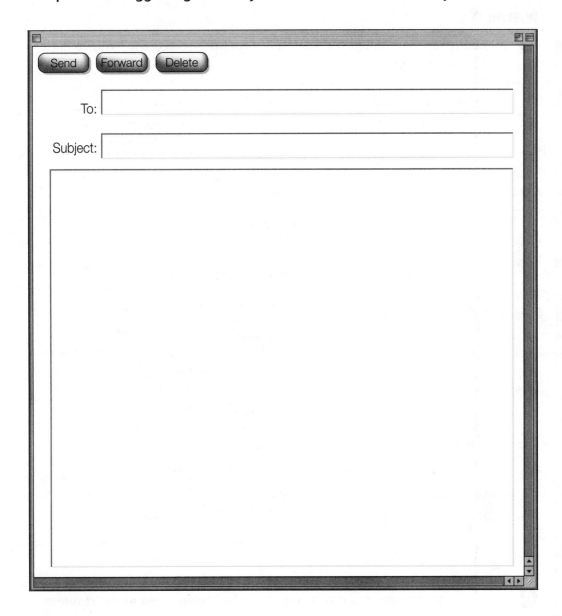

Send   Forward   Delete

To:

Subject:

REVISING

D Read over your paragraph and look for ways to improve it. Use the revising checklist on page 51 to help you. Revise your paragraph and then rewrite it.

Résumés

PREWRITING

A Two people have applied for the job of English instructor for your school. Study the résumés.

Lynn Whitnall
Plaza de la Paz, No. 2
CP 36000 Guanajuato
Gto, Mexico
Home Phone + 52 (473) 732-02-13

POSITION DESIRED

English Instructor

EDUCATION

1995 BA Spanish, New York University

EMPLOYMENT

2000–present, Spanish teacher, International
          High School
1997–2000 English Instructor, Tokyo Girls
          High School
1995–1997 Peace Corps volunteer in Colombia

OTHER

Fluent in Spanish, French, Japanese

AWARDS

Excellence in Teaching Award, 2004

Deborah Fines
42 St. James Place
Philadelphia, PA 19106

Position Desired:
English Instructor

Education:
1990–94 BA English, McGill University
1996   MA English, University of Toronto
2000   PhD Linguistics, University of Pennsylvania

Employment Experience:
2000–Present Consultant and author
1996–1998 Instructor, Intensive English Program,
          University of Vermont
1994–1995 Teaching Assistant, Linguistics
          Department, University of Pennsylvania
1993–1994 Swimming teacher
1990–1993 Server, *Chez Robert*

Publication:
English Verb Tenses, Shortman Publishing Company, 2003

Personal:
Fluent in French; competitive swimmer

B Write five sentences of contrast based on the information in the résumés.

> **EXAMPLE**
>
> *Deborah has more degrees than Lynn.*

1. _____

2. _____

3. _____

4. _____

5. _____

C Whom would you hire for the job? Write a paragraph supporting your decision.

_____

_____

_____

_____

_____

_____

D Read over your paragraph and look for ways to improve it. Use the revising checklist on page 51 to help you. Revise your paragraph and then rewrite it.

Contrasting Cultures

A Talk to a classmate from another country. Discuss the differences between eating habits (or climate, social customs, family life, education, political system, or economy) in your culture and your partner's culture. If everyone in the class is from the same country, discuss the differences between your family and your partner's family. Make a list of the differences.

_____   _____

_____   _____

_____   _____

B Write a paragraph of contrast. Use your list as a guide. Start with the biggest differences.

_____

_____

_____

_____

_____

_____

C Ask your partner for suggestions to improve your paragraph. You can also use the revising checklist on page 51 to help you. Revise your paragraph and then rewrite it.

You Be the Editor

1. The following e-mail message has nine mistakes. Find the mistakes and correct them. Then rewrite the corrected message.

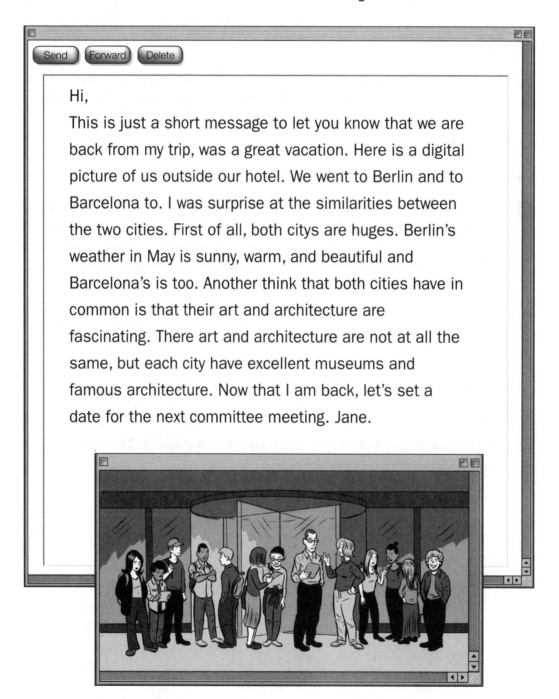

Send Forward Delete

Hi,

This is just a short message to let you know that we are back from my trip, was a great vacation. Here is a digital picture of us outside our hotel. We went to Berlin and to Barcelona to. I was surprise at the similarities between the two cities. First of all, both citys are huges. Berlin's weather in May is sunny, warm, and beautiful and Barcelona's is too. Another think that both cities have in common is that their art and architecture are fascinating. There art and architecture are not at all the same, but each city have excellent museums and famous architecture. Now that I am back, let's set a date for the next committee meeting. Jane.

2. **Read the following paragraph. It contains nine mistakes. Find the mistakes and correct them. Then rewrite the corrected paragraph.**

Francisco received a scholarship to study English in the United States. He had a difficulty time deciding whether he should attend the English program at Miami Community College in Miami, Florida, or Rocky Mountain College in Denver, Colorado. It would be a lot cheapest for him to go to the community college, but he realize that his living expenses would be a lot more high in the city. Both schools has an excellent reputation, but Rocky Mountain is a much smaller school with a best student/teacher ratio. If he goes to the community college, he will not be as far away from home and he could go home more oftener. He also thought about how he would spend his free time. He might be happier, comfortabler, and more relaxed in the mountains. Finally, decided to attend Miami Community because the temperature is warmer in Florida and he is used to warm weather and water sports.

On Your Own

Choose one of the following topics to write about. You may write about either the similarities or the differences.

- two cities you have visited
- two vacations you have taken
- two jobs you have had
- two athletic teams you like
- two types of music

CHAPTER 12

Writing about Causes and Effects

Sometimes you will need to explain a situation by analyzing its causes (reasons) and its effects (results). To write a good explanation, you have to include the cause for a situation, as well as the effect.

Analyzing a Situation for Cause and Effect

Look at the pairs of pictures below. The first picture in each pair shows a cause. The second picture shows an effect. State the cause and effect for each pair of pictures that follow.

Cause: _The boy found $100._

Effect: _The boy is happy._

1. Cause: ———————————

Effect: ———————————

2. Cause: ———————————

Effect: ———————————

(continued on next page)

3. Cause: _____   Effect: _____

_____   _____

4. Cause: _____   Effect: _____

_____   _____

Analyzing Causes

Read the model paragraph and answer the questions.

English is a difficult language to learn for several reasons. One reason is that the English spelling system is very irregular. Many English words sound the same but are spelled differently. For example, *hear* and *here* sound exactly the same, but they are spelled differently. In addition, English is difficult to learn because it has so many idioms. There are over 7,000 idioms in common use by English speakers. Last, and most importantly, English grammar is hard because it has many exceptions. For example, many English verbs are irregular. For every rule it seems that there are two exceptions. If learners know about these difficulties with English, they might feel less frustrated.

1. What is the topic sentence?

_____

2. What causes (reasons) does the author give?

_____

_____

_____

3. How are the causes organized?

_____

SIGNAL WORDS THAT INTRODUCE A CAUSE

Study the following signal words and example sentences.

because	since	due to

EXAMPLES

I took my umbrella because it was raining.
Because it was raining, I took my umbrella.

I took my umbrella since it was raining.
Since it was raining, I took my umbrella.

I took my umbrella due to the rain.
Due to the rain, I took my umbrella.

I took my umbrella because of the rain.
Because of the rain, I took my umbrella.

WRITING SENTENCES OF CAUSE

Write a sentence of cause using _because_ or _since_ for each of the sets of pictures on pages 129 and 130.

EXAMPLE

The boy is happy because he found $100.

1. _____

2. _____

3. _____

4. _____

WRITING TOPIC SENTENCES FOR PARAGRAPHS ABOUT CAUSES

Here are some examples of topic sentences for paragraphs about causes:

- I decided to move to New York for several reasons.

- The economy is doing well for three main reasons.

- There are several causes of diabetes in adults.

Write a topic sentence for the following paragraphs.

1. _____

_____

Some people move because they want to find better jobs or to advance their careers. Others are attracted to new places because the weather is better. Still others want to move to a place with less crime. Finally, people often want to move to a place with a lower cost of living. For these reasons, every year millions of people pack up and move to new places.

2. _____

_____

One reason so many American children are overweight is that they eat too much junk food that is high in calories, sugar, and fat. Another reason is that many children do not get enough exercise. Because they spend so much time sitting in front of the television set or playing computer games, they do not move around very much. Genetics is another reason that children become overweight. Children whose parents or brothers or sisters are overweight may be at an increased risk of becoming overweight themselves.

WRITING A PARAGRAPH OF CAUSES

Your teacher will put this topic sentence on the board:

The world seems to be getting smaller for several reasons.

A Think about the topic sentence. As a class, brainstorm reasons to support the topic sentence. Your teacher will write them in list form on the board. (Remember, these are just ideas, so they don't have to be in sentence form or correct order.) Copy the list here.

_____   _____

_____   _____

_____   _____

B After you have a complete list of causes, discuss them. Decide which ones should be included in the paragraph. Cross out the ones that are not relevant.

WRITING

C Write a paragraph explaining the reasons the world seems smaller. Use your list as a guide. End with what you feel is the most important reason.

_____

_____

_____

_____

_____

_____

_____

_____

REVISING

D Read over your paragraph and look for ways to improve it. Use the revising checklist on page 51 to help you. Revise your paragraph and then rewrite it.

INDIVIDUAL ACTIVITY

In this activity you will analyze an important decision that you have made in your life.

PREWRITING

A Choose one of the following topics and make a list of reasons.

- reasons I volunteered for community service
- reasons I came to this school
- reasons I chose this after-school job
- reasons I chose my computer

Decision: _____

Reasons:

_____   _____

_____   _____

_____   _____

_____   _____

WRITING

B Write a first draft of your paragraph, using your list as a guide. Remember to begin with a topic sentence.

_____

_____

_____

_____

_____

_____

_____

_____

REVISING

C Give your paragraph to one of your classmates to read. Ask him or her to make suggestions about ways to improve the paragraph. You can also use the revising checklist on page 51 to help you. Revise your paragraph and then rewrite it.

SMALL GROUP ACTIVITY

You are a business administration student. You have been asked to analyze the following case history with a group of students.

PREWRITING

A **Read the case.**

> ▶ **CASE HISTORY #6**
>
> On September 5, Michael Williams opened a small compact disc shop in the basement of the Fairfax Apartment Building. The apartment building is located on a small side street just outside of town. It is three miles away from a large shopping center that has two discount compact disc stores.
>
> Mr. Williams spent $10,000 buying CDs for his shop. Most of the CDs were rock 'n' roll. He sold each CD for $8.00. He hired three people to work as salespersons and paid them $5.50 an hour. The shop was open Monday to Friday from 1:00 to 5:00 P.M. Mr. Williams would not accept checks or credit cards.
>
> On December 19, Mr. Williams closed his shop. He put a sign on the door that said "Out of Business."

B **Discuss this case in your group. Why do you think the business failed? Make a list of the causes.**

_____   _____

_____   _____

_____   _____

_____   _____

_____   _____

_____   _____

_____   _____

Residents of the Fairfax by Age Groups

Age of Residents	Number of Residents
0–10	14
11–20	3
21–30	20
31–40	25
41–50	45
51–60	57
61 +	43

1. How can you describe the people who live in the Fairfax? What generalization can you make about the people?

_____

_____

_____

2. Can you use the information in this table to think of another cause of the failure of this business? Add it to your original list of causes.

_____

_____

_____

D Now study this table.

Number of People Who Walk Past the Store	MON	TUES	WED	THURS	FRI	SAT	SUN
In the morning 8AM–12PM	30	35	28	29	31	32	20
In the afternoon 12PM–6PM	10	12	16	15	20	70	65
In the evening 6PM–12AM	40	47	53	42	60	65	40

E Write three statements based on this table.

1. _____

2. _____

3. _____

Does the information in this table show another cause of the failure? What is it?

4. _____

F Write a first draft of a paragraph discussing the causes of the failure of Mr. Williams's compact disc shop.

_____

_____

_____

_____

_____

_____

_____

_____

REVISING

G Read over your group's paragraph and look for ways to improve it. Use the revising checklist on page 51 to help you. Revise the paragraph and then rewrite it.

Analyzing Effects

Read the model paragraph and answer the questions.

> Watching television can have several positive effects on students learning English. One effect is that students can improve their pronunciation by listening to the people on television. In addition, students can observe gestures and body language that are part of communication. Most importantly, students are exposed to a wide variety of idioms that are commonly used by English speakers.

1. What is the topic sentence?

_____

2. What effects does the author give?

_____

_____

3. What kind of order does the author use to explain the effects?

_____

SIGNAL WORDS THAT INTRODUCE AN EFFECT

Study the following signal words and example sentences.

so	thus	therefore	consequently	as a result

EXAMPLES

Laura wants to make the basketball team, *so* she practices every day.

Laura wants to make the basketball team. *Therefore,* she practices every day.
Thus,
Consequently,
As a result,

Laura wants to make the basketball team; *therefore,* she practices every day.
thus,
consequently,
as a result,

WRITING SENTENCES OF CAUSE AND EFFECT

A Look at this cartoon. Complete the sentences that follow with signal words of cause and effect.

1. There are no ice cubes in Snoopy's water, _____ he is angry.

2. There are no ice cubes in Snoopy's water; _____, he is angry.

3. There are no ice cubes in Snoopy's water. _____, he is angry.

B Write a sentence of cause and effect using *so* or *therefore* for each of the sets of pictures on pages 129 and 130.

EXAMPLE

The boy found $100; therefore, he is happy.

1. _____

2. _____

3. _____

4. _____

C Match the causes and effects. The first one has been done for you.

Effects

1. _d_ I'm going skiing today.

2. ____ We moved to the country.

3. ____ We bought a new car.

4. ____ They took an airplane.

5. ____ She doesn't eat desserts.

6. ____ The flowers in our garden died.

7. ____ He went to the dentist.

8. ____ He rides his bike to school.

9. ____ We turned on the air conditioner.

Causes

a. It was faster than the train.

b. He likes to get exercise in the morning.

c. The city was too crowded.

d. It snowed five inches last night.

e. It didn't rain enough this summer.

f. The old one used too much gas.

g. She doesn't like sweets.

h. He had a toothache.

i. It is very hot today.

Now combine the causes and effects to make new sentences. Use *so, because,* or *therefore.*

1. *It snowed five inches last night, so I'm going skiing today.*

2. _____

3. _____

4. _____

5. _____

6. _____

7. _____

8. _____

9. _____

WRITING TOPIC SENTENCES FOR PARAGRAPHS ABOUT EFFECTS

Here are some examples of topic sentences for paragraphs about effects:

- Computers have had several important effects on society.

- There are a number of consequences of global warming.

- The birth of my twin sisters has had several effects on my life.

- The flood caused several problems in our town.

Write a topic sentence for the following paragraphs.

1. _____

For one thing, there was so much snow that it was dangerous to drive and several main roads had to be closed. In addition, students had the day off because all the schools were closed. Finally, the snowstorm cost the city a lot of money to clean up.

2. _____

First of all, running increases the efficiency of the heart and lungs. Running also helps the body develop greater physical endurance. Finally, it helps the body become more mechanically efficient.

3. _____

I have to be at work earlier in the morning, and I have much more responsibility. It also means that I make more money. All things considered, this is a great opportunity and I am very happy with my new job.

RECOGNIZING IRRELEVANT SENTENCES

The following paragraphs each contain one sentence that is irrelevant. Cross out that sentence and be prepared to explain why it does not belong in the paragraph.

1. There are several reasons why many American women are waiting until they are thirty years old or older to have their first baby. Some women have good jobs and want to continue their careers. Many American couples have two children. Other women don't want the responsibility of having children until they are older. Still others are waiting until they are financially secure before they start a family. Increased personal and professional opportunities for women often result in delaying motherhood.

2. Listening to music can have many positive effects on children. For one thing, listening to music can increase verbal, emotional, and spatial intelligence. Some children prefer sports to music. It can also improve concentration and stimulate creative thinking. Finally, another positive effect of music is that it can relax children and make them feel more comfortable. Some scientists think music can even improve children's memory. Overall, it seems music is beneficial to children's learning and sense of well-being.

3. The introduction of affordable automobiles had several effects on North American society. First of all, automobiles created a more mobile society. Automobiles made it possible for people to move out of the cities and into the suburbs. Automobiles also affected the growth of new businesses. Gas stations, auto repair shops, and roadside restaurants became necessary. Railroads had a great effect on society too. In addition, new roads were built as a result of the increase in the number of cars. All of these changes meant that the automobile was transforming the lifestyle of millions of North Americans.

WRITING EFFECTS PARAGRAPHS

PREWRITING

A Your teacher will put this topic sentence on the board:

There are several effects of pollution.

B What effects can you and your classmates think of? Brainstorm a list of effects. Your teacher will write them in list form on the board. (Remember, these are just ideas, so they don't have to be in sentence form or correct order.) Copy the list here.

_____   _____

_____   _____

_____   _____

C After you have a complete list of effects, discuss them. Decide which should be included in the paragraph. Cross out the ones that are not strong or relevant.

D Write a paragraph about the effects of pollution, using your list as a guide. End with what you feel is the most important effect.

_____

_____

_____

_____

_____

_____

_____

_____

REVISING

E Read over your paragraph and look for ways to improve it. Use the revising checklist on page 51 to help you. Revise your paragraph and then rewrite it.

ANALYZING EFFECTS

The Effects of Sugar

PREWRITING

A Read the following list of facts about white sugar.

- robs the body of vitamin B

- causes tooth decay

- interferes with calcium metabolism

- contributes to hardening of arteries

WRITING

B Use the list to write a paragraph about the effects of white sugar on the human body. Begin with a topic sentence.

_____

_____

_____

_____

_____

_____

_____

_____

C Read over your paragraph and look for ways to improve it. Use the revising checklist on page 51 to help you. Revise your paragraph and then rewrite it.

The Effects of a Decision

PREWRITING

A Choose one of the following topics and make a list of the effects that decision has had on your life.

- volunteering to help others
- learning to play a musical instrument
- buying a computer
- picking a school
- coming to an English-speaking country

_____   _____

_____   _____

_____   _____

WRITING

B Write a first draft of your paragraph, using your list as a guide. Remember to begin with a topic sentence.

_____

_____

_____

_____

_____

_____

_____

REVISING

C Give your paragraph to one of your classmates to read. Ask him or her to make suggestions about ways to improve the paragraph. You can use the revising checklist on page 51 to help you. Revise your paragraph and then rewrite it.

SMALL GROUP ACTIVITY

PREWRITING

A Read the following information.

> Acton is a small town in the Midwest. It has a population of 2,500. It is a safe, quiet, and clean place to live. Most of the people have lived there all their lives and know each other very well. The town has not changed very much in the past one hundred years.
>
> Last month, Stanley Manufacturing decided to open a large factory in Acton. This will bring many new people to the community. Some people are worried about the negative effects the new factory will have on the town. Other people are excited about the positive effects the new factory will have on Acton.

B In small groups make predictions about the impact the new factory will have on Acton. Make a list of all the possible effects you can think of.

Positive	Negative
more jobs	*pollution*

WRITING

C Choose one of the groups below.

1. You and other conservative residents don't want Acton to change. On a separate piece of paper, write a paragraph predicting the negative effects the factory will have on the town.

2. You and other progressive residents are open to changes in your community. On a separate piece of paper, write a paragraph predicting the positive effects the new factory will have on the town.

REVISING

D Read over your group's paragraph and look for ways to improve it. Use the revising checklist on page 51 to help you. Revise your paragraph and then rewrite it.

PAIR ACTIVITY

PREWRITING

A Look at the diagram below. It shows how plants and animals depend on each other in a farm pond. Discuss the diagram with a classmate. Imagine that you have been asked to write a short explanation of this diagram for a children's science magazine.

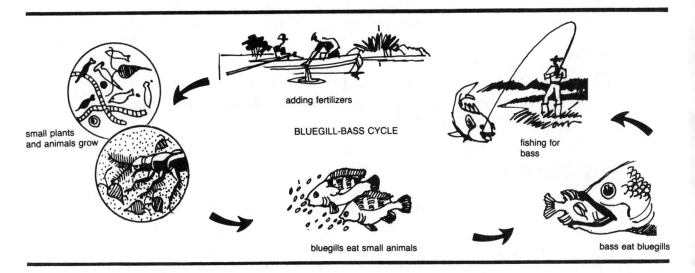

small plants and animals grow

adding fertilizers

BLUEGILL-BASS CYCLE

fishing for bass

bluegills eat small animals

bass eat bluegills

B Make a list of the effects that plants and animals in the pond have on each other.

_____   _____

_____   _____

_____   _____

C Write a paragraph about the ecological relationships that are shown in the diagram. Begin with a topic sentence.

_____

_____

_____

_____

_____

_____

_____

_____

REVISING

D Read over your paragraph with your partner and look for ways to improve it. Use the revising checklist on page 51 to help you. Revise your paragraph and then rewrite it.

JUST FOR FUN

Match the questions in column A with the answers in column B.

A	B
1. ____ Why did the man cross the street?	**a.** His head is so far from his body.
2. ____ Why did the man throw the clock out the window?	**b.** They live in schools.
	c. He wanted to see time fly.
3. ____ Why does the giraffe have such a long neck?	**d.** He wanted to get to the other side.
4. ____ Why did the man tiptoe past the medicine cabinet?	**e.** He didn't want to wake up the sleeping pills.
5. ____ Why are fish smarter than insects?	**f.** It has the largest number of stories.
6. ____ Why is a library the tallest building?	

You Be the Editor

Read the following article. It contains seven mistakes. Find the mistakes and correct them. Then rewrite the corrected article.

DEADLY SURPRISE TORNADO

August 3. The tornado that hit kansas today surprised even the weather forecasters. The violent winds blowed over 200 miles per hour. Much crops were destroyed by the storm. Hundreds of people lost his homes or offices because of the high winds and heavy rains. The Red Cross estimates that the killer storm caused many injuries. Also, million of dollars worth of farm animals were killed due to the tornado. will take the people of Kansas many time to recover from the effects of this tornado.

On Your Own

Choose one of these topics and write a paragraph.

- causes or effects of immigrating to a new country
- causes or effects of overeating
- causes or effects of a recent economic or political situation in your country or a country you know well

Writing Personal and Business Letters

In this chapter you will learn how to write two kinds of letters—personal letters and business letters.

Personal Letters

Personal letters are often called "friendly letters." They are letters that you write to a friend or relative. Personal letters include information about you, and ask questions about how your friend or relative is doing. Personal letters are informal and do not have to be typed. There are five main parts to a personal letter. The parts are labeled on the model letter below.

date | *January 3, 2006*

Dear Daniel, | greeting

Thank you very much for the wonderful week I spent with you and your family. Your mother is such a terrific cook! I think I must have gained ten pounds in just the seven days I spent with you. I really appreciate your taking me around and showing me so many places. You are lucky to live in such an interesting area. I hope that soon you will be able to visit my part of the country. Thank you again for a wonderful time. Let's keep in touch. | message

Best regards, | closing

Mauricio | signature

Remember these guidelines when you write a personal letter:

- The date goes in the upper right corner. (The month is capitalized, and a comma goes between the day and the year.)
- The greeting (Dear _____) is followed by a comma.
- The closing (often "Love" in personal letters) is followed by a comma.

Use the following form for the envelope of a personal letter:

Mauricio Graham
327 South 2nd Street
Philadelphia, PA 19012

Mr. Daniel Lourie
52 Main Street
Conby, OR 99106

Don't forget:

- The return address of the person who writes the letter goes in the upper left corner.

- The address of the person who will receive the letter goes in the center of the envelope.

- The stamp goes in the upper right corner.

WRITING A PERSONAL LETTER

Write a personal letter to a friend you haven't seen recently. Tell him or her what is new in your life. Also, ask some questions about his or her life.

_____

_____

_____

_____

_____

_____

_____

_____

_____

_____

Write a short letter to each of the following people. Bring your finished letters to class in properly addressed envelopes.

- A friend. Invite him or her to come visit you.

- Your aunt. Thank her for the gift she sent you.

- Your parents. Tell them about an important decision you have made.

Exchange letters with a classmate and write short responses to the letters.

Business Letters

Business letters are more formal than personal letters. They are usually written to someone you do not know. You might write a business letter to request information or to inform someone about a problem. Look at the model business letter. There are six parts to a business letter. There are several acceptable formats you can use for a business letter, but the block format shown here is the most common. In the block format, all parts begin on the left margin.

177 Atlantic Avenue
Boston, Massachusetts 02140   *heading*
April 22, 2005

Director of Admissions
Harvard University   *inside address*
Cambridge, Massachusetts 02138

Dear Sir or Madam: *greeting*

I am a senior at Springfield Academy and I am interested in attending Harvard University to study business. Please send me the appropriate application forms and any information you have about the undergraduate business program. I will also need information *message* about TOEFL requirements because English is not my native language.

I look forward to hearing from you.
   closing
Sincerely,

Hasan Halkali | signature

Hasan Halkali

Remember these guidelines for writing business letters:

- Use a colon after the greeting.

- Identify yourself and state the purpose of your letter at the beginning. Go directly to the point. Be brief and clear.

- Type business letters if possible.

- Do not ask personal information (age, health, family) of the person you are writing to.

- Do not use slang, informal phrases, or contractions.

IDENTIFYING FORMAL AND INFORMAL PHRASES

In each pair of sentences or phrases below, one should be used only in informal letters. The other one is appropriate for formal letters. Put an _F_ in front of the one that is formal and an _I_ in front of the one that is informal.

1. _____ I'm really sorry about what happened.

   _____ I would like to apologize for the inconvenience this caused you.

2. _____ I look forward to hearing from you soon.

   _____ I can't wait to hear from you.

3. _____ Dear Julie,

   _____ Dear Mrs. Brody:

4. _____ Yours truly,

   _____ Love,

5. _____ I will call you Monday morning.

   _____ I'll give you a call next week.

6. _____ I appreciate your help in this matter.

   _____ Thanks a lot for helping me.

WRITING A BUSINESS LETTER

A Read the advertisement for the space show at the planetarium.

JOURNEY TO THE EDGE OF THE UNIVERSE!

Rose Center for Earth and Space
American Museum of Natural History
175 Central Park W.
New York, NY 10024

ORDER TICKETS FOR THE SPACE SHOW!

Tickets include admission to the Museum.

DAILY SHOW TIMES	PRICES	
11:00 A.M.	Adults	$22.00
1:00 P.M.	Children (under 12)	$13.00
2:00 P.M.	Seniors/Students	$16.50
3:30 P.M.		
4:30 P.M.		

<u>Fridays Only</u>

5:30 P.M.
6:30 P.M.

B Write a letter requesting tickets. In your letter you will need to state the following:

- the date of the show you want to attend
- the time you want to see the show
- the number of tickets you want and their prices
- whether you are including your credit card number or a personal check

_____

_____

_____

_____

_____

_____

_____

_____

_____

_____

_____

_____

_____

_____

_____

_____

C Read your letter again. Consider the following questions and make corrections if necessary.

- Have you included both a heading and an inside address? Are they in the proper places?

- Is there a colon after the greeting?

- Is your letter direct and to the point?

- Is the closing followed by a comma?

- Did you sign your letter?

D Revise your letter and then rewrite it.

A Write about one of the following situations.

- Write to a college admissions office asking for information.

- Write to a radio station requesting more information about a product you heard advertised.

- Write a letter to a magazine publisher stating that you ordered a magazine subscription three months ago but haven't received a magazine yet.

- Write a letter of importance to you.

B When you have finished the letter, review the questions in part C on page 154. Make corrections if necessary.

C Bring your finished letter to class in a properly addressed envelope. (Use the same format for a business letter envelope that you use for a personal letter envelope.) Exchange letters with a classmate and give each other suggestions for making your letters clearer.

LETTERS OF COMPLAINT

A Imagine yourself in the following situation:

Two weeks ago you called the person who lives above you in your apartment building. You were upset because he plays his stereo so loudly. He plays it very loudly all day long so it bothers you when you are trying to study. He also plays it late at night when you are trying to sleep. When you spoke with him on the phone, he said that he would try to keep the volume lower. The first few days it was better, but now it is becoming a problem again. Also, you are trying to study for your final exam. It is very difficult because of the constant noise.

B Write a polite letter to him asking him to please be more considerate.

_____

_____

_____

_____

_____

_____

_____

_____

C It is now one week later and the noise has gotten even worse. You are furious. Write an angry letter to your landlord threatening to break your lease and move out if he or she does not do something about the noise. Since this is a business letter, don't forget the heading and the inside address. Remember to type the final copy of a business letter.

_____

_____

_____

_____

_____

_____

_____

_____

_____

_____

_____

_____

_____

_____

1. **Read the following personal letter. It contains seven mistakes. Correct the mistakes and rewrite the corrected letter.**

January 10, 2006

Dear Isabelle:

I just visited the Morgan Motor Company factory in Malvern, england, and I felt like I was back in the 1920s. There are computers and other modern equipment, but I soon realized that most things have not changed. Morgans is still made the old-fashioned way. Each one is build by hand, so no two are exactly alike, and only about ten cars are made per week. That's why there is over a five-year waiting list for a new one. Morgans don't have power steering, a power brakes, or a radio. But, they do have a loyals fan club. Morgan lovers can talk for hours about the thrill of feeling every bump in the road, of listening to the roar of the wind, and of smelling the sweet perfume of burning oil as they drive along. I put my name at the waiting list for a new Morgan!

Love,

Jackson

2. **Read the following business letter. It contains eight mistakes. Correct the mistakes and rewrite the corrected letter.**

535 West Boulevard

San Diego, CA 92101

March 2, 2006

San Diego Zoo

P.O. Box 120551

San Diego, CA 92112–0551

Dear Sir or Madam,

Our class wishes to arrange a visit to the San diego Zoo. In our biology

class, we have learn about endangered species such as giant pandas,

tiger, and condors. We know that the zoo promotes the conservation of

threatened species. it has a large research program to protect species and

habitats in the wild. The students in my class would appreciate hearing

about what members of your staff are doing to educate the public. Please

let me know how to plan our trip. I look forward to hearing from you.

sincerely

Gerda Steiner

Gerda Steiner

CHAPTER 14

Writing Summaries

Summaries

Summaries require a special kind of writing. A good summary gives only main ideas. It does not include details. Before you begin to write a summary, you should think about *who, when, where, why, what,* and *how.*

A **Read the article below. As you read, underline only the main ideas.**

An Alaskan Dog Hero

A husky named Balto became famous in 1925 when he led a dog team into Nome, Alaska, to rescue the children there from a deadly disease. The children of Nome were in danger from a diphtheria epidemic. The serum needed to stop the disease was in Anchorage, about a thousand miles away. The airplane that could bring the medicine to Nome was out of service for the winter. The only way to deliver the serum was by using sled dogs.

Several dog-sled teams were used in the life-or-death race. A train brought the serum from Anchorage to Nenana, where the first dog-sled team picked up the medicine. The sled dogs traveled in blizzard conditions over ice and across dangerous waters. News of the race was reported throughout the world. On the last leg of the journey, Balto led his brave dog team into Nome. The run had taken only six days.

The team driver told reporters of Balto's heroic actions: "I couldn't see the trail. . . . I gave Balto, my lead dog, his head and trusted him. He never once faltered. It was Balto who led the way. The credit is his." Balto was honored for his heroic action with a life-size bronze sculpture that stands outdoors in New York City's Central Park. Balto is shown wearing his dog-sled harness. Another statue of the canine hero is in downtown Anchorage. Every year a sled-dog race called the Iditarod honors the memory of Balto's great historic race.

B **Read the statements about the story. Put *MI* next to sentences that are main ideas. Put *D* next to sentences that give details.**

1. _____ Balto became famous in 1925 after a race to save the children of Nome, Alaska, from a deadly disease.

2. _____ The serum that could stop the outbreak was in Anchorage.

3. _____ A plane that could have made the journey was out of service.

4. _____ The only way to get serum to the children was by using dog-sled teams.

5. _____ The serum was transported by train from Anchorage to Nenana.

6. _____ The dogs had to travel in blizzard conditions.

7. _____ News of the race was reported throughout the world.

8. _____ Balto led the final dog team into Nome.

9. ___ Balto was honored for his heroic action with a sculpture.

10. ___ Balto's statue shows him wearing his dog-sled harness.

C **Complete the summary below.**

A husky named _____ (who) became known around the world in

_____ (when) for saving the children of _____

(where). The dog and his team brought _____ (what) to prevent an

epidemic of _____ (what).

WRITING A SUMMARY

PREWRITING

A **Read the following article about endangered animals.**

> ▶ WHY DO SOME ANIMALS DIE OUT?

It is natural for species of animals to become extinct over millions of years. But, in the past 200 years, humans have caused the process to speed up. Between 1996 and 2004 the total number of threatened animal species increased from 5,205 to 7,180. Recent surveys show that 23 percent (nearly one in four) of mammal species and more than 20 percent (one in five) of the world's bird species are threatened with extinction. In most cases this is a result of human activity. How are people accelerating the process of animal extinction?

First of all, people threaten the survival of animal species by destroying their habitats. As human populations grow, people keep building houses and factories in fields and woods. As they spread over the land, they destroy animals' homes. If the animals can't find a place to live, they die out. More than 20 Hawaiian bird species have become extinct since 1500. Thirty-two species that breed on Hawaiian islands are now on the endangered list.

Overhunting is another way that humans are causing some animals to become extinct. In some parts of the world, the parts of rare animals are worth a lot of money. For example, some people will pay more than $1,000 for a single rhino horn. This encourages hunters to kill rhinos even though they face extinction. Other animals that are threatened with extinction from overhunting include the blue whale, the mountain gorilla, and the cheetah. In October 2005, there were only 60 cheetahs left in the world.

Humans are also polluting the air, water, and soil. The effect of pollution on animal species can be complicated. For example, when waste from factories is dumped into rivers, the rivers become polluted. The fish that live in the river are poisoned and many of them die. In addition, birds that eat the poisoned fish become poisoned themselves. Once they are poisoned, these birds cannot lay strong, healthy eggs. Fewer and fewer new birds are born. So far, no animals have become extinct because of pollution. But some, such as the brown pelican, have become rare and may die out.

(continued on next page)

Finally, when humans introduce new species into certain environments, the animals that already live there become threatened and face extinction. For example, when European settlers brought rabbits and foxes to Australia, they killed off many native Australian animals, including the bandicoot. The rabbits and foxes adapted to the Australian environment very quickly and multiplied rapidly. Eventually, the foxes hunted and killed many bandicoots for food. The rabbits took over the bandicoot habitats. Now, the Southern Brown Bandicoot is listed as an endangered species in New South Wales in southeast Australia.

B **Now answer the following questions.**

1. What is the article about?

_____

2. Why is it happening?

_____

3. Who is responsible?

_____

4. When is it happening?

_____

WRITING

C **Write a one-paragraph summary of the article. State the main idea of the article in the first sentence. Answer the questions *what, when,* and *how* in the rest of the paragraph.**

_____

_____

_____

_____

_____

_____

_____

_____

REVISING

D **Did you answer all of the questions in part B? Look at the revising checklist on page 51. Exchange papers with a partner and edit each other's papers. Did you both include the same information? If not, what were the differences? Revise your paragraph and then rewrite it.**

PREWRITING

A Read this short news article.

Category 5 Hurricane Strikes

Hurricane Katrina, the first Category 5 hurricane of the season, struck the Central Gulf Coast near New Orleans, Louisiana, on August 29. Damage to the coastal regions of Louisiana, Mississippi, and Alabama, as well as to other areas, has made this storm the most destructive natural disaster in American history.

Several sections of the levee system that protects New Orleans collapsed and caused the city to be flooded by waters from Lake Pontchartrain. In some parts of the city, the water was 20 to 25 feet deep. About 80 percent of New Orleans was reported under water at the height of the storm.

Winds of up to 175 miles per hour struck the area. Many homes and businesses were severely damaged or destroyed. Hundreds of thousands of people lost everything they owned. Communications were knocked out, which made relief and rescue difficult. The hurricane left about five million people without power.

People were ordered to leave their homes. Over a million people were forced to move by the storm. Nearly half a million were evacuated to nearby states, chiefly Texas, Georgia, and Arkansas. People who were unable to leave were kept in shelters under very

difficult conditions. More than 1,100 people lost their lives.

The total damages have been estimated at $200 billion. Because a number of oil refineries are in the Gulf Coast region, the storm interrupted oil supply and led to a rise in energy costs. The contamination of food and drinking water raised concerns about health problems in the area.

The American public responded to the disaster by sending generous donations as well as volunteers. More than seventy countries around the world offered aid to the United States.

PREWRITING

B Make a list of the important facts in the article. Try to include *who, what, when, where, why,* and *how* on your list.

_____   _____

_____   _____

_____   _____

_____   _____

_____   _____

C Study your list. Make sure you have included only the main ideas. Cross out any items on your list that are details.

WRITING

D Write a short, one-paragraph summary of the article.

_____

_____

_____

_____

_____

_____

REVISING

E Compare your summary with some of your classmates' summaries. Have you included too much information? Did you miss an important idea? Revise your summary paragraph and then rewrite it.

On Your Own

Find an article in a book, magazine, or newspaper. Read it carefully and write a one-paragraph summary of it. Bring the article and your summary to class. Exchange summaries with a classmate and give each other suggestions for improving the summary.

Answering Test Questions

Teachers and professors often ask you to answer questions in paragraph form on tests. There are several important things to remember when answering test questions.

- Read the entire question carefully.

- Make sure you understand exactly what information you are being asked to write about (reasons, definitions, etc.).

- Plan your answer.

- Budget your time.

BEGINNING THE ESSAY

You will find that the easiest way to begin your essay is to change the question to a statement and use this statement as your topic sentence. (Often the "question" is not written in question form, but in the imperative form.) Study the example.

EXAMPLE

Question: Discuss why Americans move so often.

Topic sentence: *There are many reasons why Americans move often.*

Change the following essay questions into topic sentences.

1. **Question:** Discuss why many women are waiting until after they are thirty years old to have children.

Topic Sentence: _____

_____

2. **Question:** Discuss the effects of radiation on the human body.

Topic Sentence: _____

_____

3. **Question:** Explain the reasons ice hockey is a dangerous sport.

Topic Sentence: _____

_____

4. **Question:** Explain the importance of John F. Kennedy in American history.

Topic Sentence: _____

_____

5. **Question:** Discuss the reasons why so many tourists visit Brazil.

Topic Sentence: _____

_____

6. **Question:** Explain the reasons for the popularity of video games.

Topic Sentence: _____

_____

(continued on next page)

7.   **Question:**   Discuss the advantages and disadvantages of solar energy.

     Topic Sentence: _____

_____

8.   **Question:**   Describe the four kinds of clouds.

     Topic Sentence: _____

_____

9.   **Question:**   Describe the four stages involved in cell division.

     Topic Sentence: _____

_____

THE PARTS OF THE TEST ANSWER

Read the following question and student response. Then answer the questions that follow.

Question:
What are the three stages of sending a spacecraft into orbit?

Student Answer:
    There are three stages involved in sending a spacecraft into orbit. First, the Stage One Rocket is used for the blastoff, but it is only used for two and a half minutes. When the spacecraft reaches a speed of 6,000 miles per hour and an altitude of 40 miles, this rocket drops off into the sea. Then, the Stage Two Rocket is used, but only for about six minutes, because it drops off when the spacecraft reaches a speed of 14,000 miles per hour and an altitude of 110 miles. Finally, during the third stage, the spacecraft goes into orbit. The Stage Three Rocket is used for two minutes, or until the spacecraft reaches a speed of 17,500 miles per hour and an altitude of 120 miles.

1. What is the topic sentence?

_____

2. Does it restate the question?

_____

3. Underline the signal words the student used.

_____

4. What specific information (details such as numbers and times) did the student include?

_____   _____

_____   _____

_____   _____

WRITING A RESPONSE TO A TEST QUESTION

Discuss the many similarities between the eye and the camera. Base your answer on the following information.

The eye

The human eye has an iris that gets bigger or smaller to let in the right amount of light. It also has a lens that focuses the light into a clear picture. In the eye, light forms a picture on the retina. The nerve cells in the retina send a picture message to the brain. The picture the brain receives is upside down. The brain then interprets the message so that what you see is right side up.

The camera

The camera has a diaphragm that gets bigger or smaller to let in the right amount of light. It also has a lens that focuses the light into a clear picture. In a camera, light forms a picture on film. The picture is upside down on the film.

_____

_____

_____

_____

_____

_____

_____

_____

Read the following paragraph about web logs. It contains ten mistakes. Find the mistakes and correct them. Then rewrite the paragraph.

A web log (also known as a "blog") is a journal someone keep online. When a blog is updated, the most recent postings appears at the top of page. The people who keep blogs are call "bloggers." Blogs cover different topics. Many were about current events or politics. Some blogs allow readers to post there own comments. Experts say that the use of web logs is growing dramaticaly. One survey says that 30.000 to 40,000 new blogs is created very day. One service which tracks web logs says there are close to 8 million blogs, double the number tracking in October 2004.

CHAPTER 3—You Be the Editor (page 30)

T
~~t~~hroughout history, people have found it necessary to do

I
mathematical computations, and keep accounts. ~~i~~n early times, we

T
used groups of sticks or stones to help make calculations. ~~t~~hen the

         C   *T*
abacus was developed in ~~c~~hina. ~~t~~hese simple methods represent the

                A
beginnings of data processing. ~~a~~s computational needs became more

                               O
complicated, we developed more advanced technologies. ~~o~~ne example

               B   *P*
is the first simple adding machine that ~~b~~laise ~~p~~ascal developed in

F   *A*
~~f~~rance in 1642. ~~a~~nother example is the first machine that would do

                 C   *B*
calculations and print out results, which ~~c~~harles ~~b~~abbage designed in

E   *I*
~~e~~ngland in the 1830s. ~~i~~n the middle of the twentieth century,

          U   *P*
researchers at the ~~u~~niversity of ~~p~~ennsylvania built the first successful

        T
electronic computer. ~~t~~oday, of course, we have the computer to perform

all kinds of advanced mathematical computations.

CHAPTER 4—You Be the Editor (page 38)

       s   *likes*   *s*
Erik enjoy‸ many types of sports. He ~~is liking~~ team sport‸ such as

basketball, soccer, and baseball. He also plays traditional~~s~~ individual

                               His
sports like racquetball and golf. ~~his~~ favorite sports involve danger as

        excitement   *‸*
well as ~~exciting~~. He loves extreme skiing and skydiving.

CHAPTER 5—You Be the Editor (page 45)

Our garage is ~~use~~ *used* as a storage area. At the back of the garage, there

are two big~~s~~ trash bins filled with old newspapers and magazines to

be recycled. Against the right wall is an old workbench covered with

tool*s*, bricks, and wood. On the opposite wall, we *are* storing an old TV, a

folding cot, a fan, and my ~~sisters~~ *sister's* tricycle. ~~Its~~ *It's* no surprise that our car is

parked in the driveway.

CHAPTER 7—You Be the Editor (page 66)

New Guidelines for Diets   3234

In 2005 the government announced new guidelines to help people ~~loose~~ *lose* weight. Tommy Thompson, the Secretary of Health and ~~h~~*H*uman Services, said, "Nearly two-thirds of American*s* are overweight or obese, and more than 50 percent of us do not get the recommended amount *of* physical activity." Extra weight and lack of exercise can raise the risk of cancer, diabetes, heart disease, and stroke. The guidelines emphasize~~s~~ healthier eating and physical activity. People are ~~advise~~ *advised* to eat more fruits, vegetables, and whole grains and to choose poultry, fish, and meats without a lot of fat. They are encouraged to get at least thirty minutes of exercise every day. Each person need*s* to make the right food and exercise choices.

CHAPTER 8—You Be the Editor (page 78)

To remove a tick and avoid infections, follow these steps. First, use
fine-point tweezers to get hold of ∧ *the* tick as close to the skin as you
can. Then, gently pull the ticks out without squeezing ~~it's~~ *its* body.
After that, place the tick in a small container∧ ~~So~~ *so* that it can
be tested by a lab or a veterinarian. Next, wash ~~you~~ *your* hands and clean
the site of the bite and the tweezer∧*s* with disinfectant. Finally, watch for
signs ~~for~~ *of* illness and call your doctor to find out if you ~~needed~~ need
treatment.

CHAPTER 9—You Be the Editor (page 91)

My dog, Bette, is missing. She is a small black poodle with brown~~s~~
eyes. ~~her~~ *Her* hair is short and curly. Bette weighs eight pounds and is
about one and a half ~~foots~~ *feet* long. She has a short tail, long, floppy ears,
and small feet. She is wear∧*ing* a silver collar with an ID tag on it. She is
very friendly around people and love∧*s* children. I have had Bette for six
years, since she was a puppy, and I miss her very much. I am offering
a $50 reward for anyone ~~which~~ *who* finds Bette. Please call me at
305-555-7671.

Dear Editor:

In my opinion, it is important for women with small

childrens to work outside of the home. First of all, it is ~~to~~ *too*

difficult to be with little kids all day. Womens needs a break

from ~~there~~ *their* kids. Also, a woman who has a career can offer her

children mores. It is the quality of time that mothers spend

with ~~there~~ *their* children that ~~are~~ *is* important.

Sincerely,

Lisa Harris

Send Forward Delete

Hi,

This is just a short message to let you know that we are

back from ~~my~~ *our* trip~~,~~ *. It* was a great vacation. Here is a digital

picture of us outside our hotel. We went to Berlin and to

Barcelona ~~to~~ *too*. I was surprise*d* at the similarities between

the two cities. First of all, both ~~citys~~ *cities* are huge~~s~~. Berlin's

weather in May is sunny, warm, and beautiful and

Barcelona's is too. Another ~~think~~ *thing* that both cities have in

common is that their art and architecture are

fascinating. ~~There~~ *Their* art and architecture are not at all the

same, but each city ~~have~~ *has* excellent museums and

famous architecture. Now that I am back, let's set a

date for the next committee meeting. Jane.

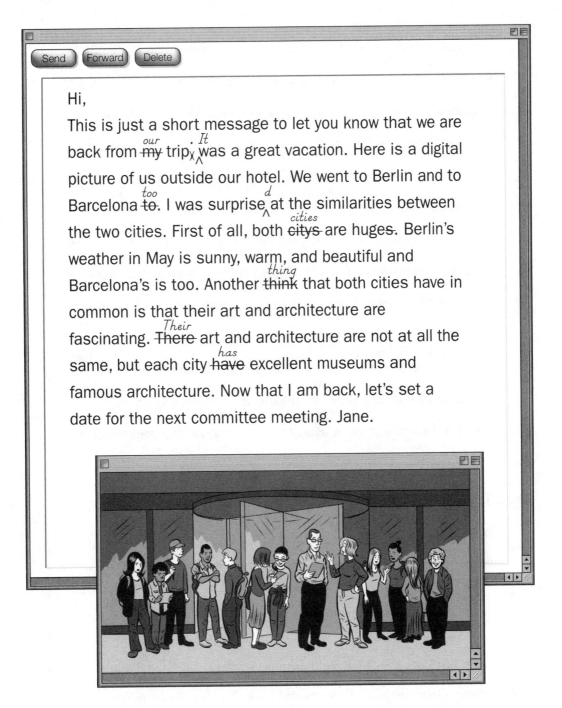

CHAPTER 11—You Be the Editor (page 127)

Francisco received a scholarship to study English in the United States.

difficult

He had a ~~difficulty~~ time deciding whether he should attend the English

program at Miami Community College in Miami, Florida, or Rocky

cheaper

Mountain College in Denver, Colorado. It would be a lot ~~cheapest~~ for

d

him to go to the community college, but he realize‸ that his living

higher   *have*

expenses would be a lot ~~more high~~ in the city. Both schools ~~has~~ an

excellent reputation, but Rocky Mountain is a much smaller school with

better

a ~~best~~ student/teacher ratio. If he goes to the community college, he

will not be as far away from home and he could go home more often~~er~~.

He also thought about how he would spend his free time. He might be

more comfortable   *he*

happier, ~~comfortabler~~, and more relaxed in the mountains. Finally,‸

decided to attend Miami Community because the temperature is

warmer in Florida and he is used to warm weather and water sports.

CHAPTER 12—You Be the Editor (page 147)

DEADLY SURPRISE TORNADO

Kansas

August 3. The tornado that hit ~~kansas~~ today surprised even the weather

blew   *Many*

forecasters. The violent winds ~~blowed~~ over 200 miles per hour. ~~Much~~

their

crops were destroyed by the storm. Hundreds of people lost ~~his~~ homes or

offices because of the high winds and heavy rains. The Red Cross

s

estimates that the killer storm caused many injuries. Also, million‸ of

It

dollars worth of farm animals were killed due to the tornado. ‸ will take

much

the people of Kansas ~~many~~ time to recover from the effects of this

tornado.

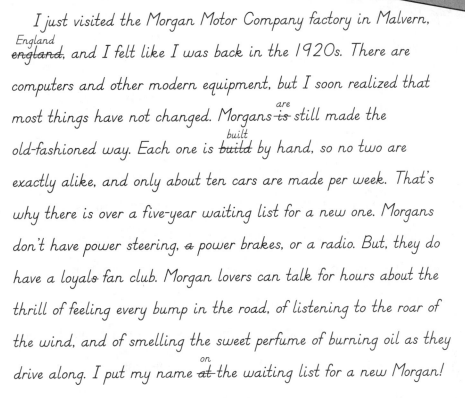

January 10, 2006

Dear Isabelle∧

    I just visited the Morgan Motor Company factory in Malvern,

England
~~england~~, and I felt like I was back in the 1920s. There are

computers and other modern equipment, but I soon realized that

are
most things have not changed. Morgans ~~is~~ still made the

built
old-fashioned way. Each one is ~~build~~ by hand, so no two are

exactly alike, and only about ten cars are made per week. That's

why there is over a five-year waiting list for a new one. Morgans

don't have power steering, ~~a~~ power brakes, or a radio. But, they do

have a loyal~~s~~ fan club. Morgan lovers can talk for hours about the

thrill of feeling every bump in the road, of listening to the roar of

the wind, and of smelling the sweet perfume of burning oil as they

on
drive along. I put my name ~~at~~ the waiting list for a new Morgan!

        Love,

        Jackson

535 West Boulevard

San Diego, CA 92101

March 2, 2006

San Diego Zoo

P.O. Box 120551

San Diego, CA 92112–0551

Dear Sir or Madam ~~x~~ *:*

    Our class wishes to arrange a visit to the San ~~diego~~ *D* Zoo. In our biology

class, we have ~~learn~~ *learned* about endangered species such as giant pandas,

tiger *s*, and condors. We know that the zoo promotes the conservation of

threatened species. ~~it~~ *I* has a large research program to protect ~~speeces~~ *species* and

habitats in the wild. The students in my class would appreciate hearing

about what members of your staff are doing to educate the public. Please

let me know how to plan our trip. I look forward to hearing from you.

~~sincerely~~ *S*

Gerda Steiner

Gerda Steiner

A web log (also known as a "blog") is a journal someone keep~s~

online. When a blog is updated, the most recent postings appear~s~

at the top of *the* ~∧~ page. The people who keep blogs are called "bloggers."

Blogs cover different topics. Many ~~were~~ *are* about current events or

politics. Some blogs allow readers to post ~~there~~ *their* own comments.

Experts say that the use of web logs is growing ~~dramaticaly.~~ *dramatically.*

One survey says that ~~30.000~~ *30,000* to 40,000 new blogs ~~is~~ *are* created ~~very~~ *every*

day. One service which tracks web logs says there are close to 8

million blogs, double the number ~~tracking~~ *tracked* in October 2004.